The Childhood of Christianity

The Childhood of Christianity

Étienne Trocmé

SCM PRESS LTD

Translated by John Bowden from the French
L'Enfance du Christianisme, by Étienne Trocmé,
published 1997 by Éditions Noêsis, 12 rue de
Savoie, Paris VIᵉ.

0 334 02709 8

First published 1997 by
SCM Press Ltd
9–17 St Albans Place London N1 0NX

Typeset by Regent Typesetting, London

Printed in Great Britain by
Biddles Ltd, Guildford and King's Lynn

Contents

Preface

Around 125 CE, in the period when the Kushana empire was reviving the expansion of Buddhism towards central Asia and China, the Parthian and Roman empires, which shared between themselves the world from India to the Atlantic Ocean, began to become aware of the establishment on their respective territories of the adherents of a new religion. These were called 'Christians' in the West and 'Nazarenes' in the East. This was still a tiny minority, amounting to perhaps 100,000 persons, dispersed in several hundred local groups which were not co-ordinated by any institution. Just under half of these groups spoke Aramaic; the rest spoke Greek, and over three-quarters of a century had produced a popular literature for which their Aramaic-speaking brothers had no equivalent.

The unity of these groups, of which their members were very aware, derived from the fact that they all claimed to go back to a certain Jesus of Nazareth, who had been executed in Jerusalem by the Roman authorities a century earlier. This messenger from God had, they said, been recalled to life by God, and that justified his being given the most extraordinary titles like Prophet, much prized in the East; God's Anointed (= Messiah in the East, Christ in the West); Lord, formerly reserved for God; or Son of God. They awaited his glorious return, which would be the occasion of a last judgment on all humankind. By means of cuts or recourse to subtle interpretation, the holy books of the Jews were understood as the announcement of this figure at the end of time.

These Christian groups had in fact recently been detached from Judaism, the religion of the Jewish people, which the two empires treated with a certain respect. On both sides of the frontier the Jews were an important minority, probably approaching ten per cent of the total population. They were an active element in economic and intellectual life. Generally submissive to the authorities, at times they would revolt, when their way of life seemed to be threatened. The Jewish War of 66–74 in Palestine, the Jewish uprising based in Cyrenaica between 115 and 117, and that of 132–135 led by Bar Kochba, show the degree to which the Jews were prone to flare up in defence of their Law and their privileges. To avoid these violent crises as far as possible, the two empires had in fact granted them a privileged status. It had sometimes been put in question but had lasted thus far.

Because of this, the Christians had no interest in separating from Judaism. Apart from some extremists, the idea did not even occur to them, so much did they feel an integral part of the Jewish people. The reason why the separation nevertheless took place was that after the destruction of the Jerusalem Temple in 70, Judaism underwent a profound change. Deprived of its cult and its sanctuary, and threatened with disintegration, it owed its survival solely to a radical reform launched by a school of Pharisaic rabbis whose ideas had been imposed on almost the whole of the Diaspora in the space of twenty years. In 90, agreement had thus been reached among the great majority of synagogues to eliminate from the Jewish communities all the nonconformists who rebelled against the doctrine of the reformers. The Christians formed part of these.

Thus excluded, the Christians had had some difficulty in finding a new equilibrium. They had had to discover that their groups could exist by themselves. They had had to become aware of their specific character, to get used to the idea that they were the vehicles of a new religion, to seek to organize themselves in order to survive. This was a complex task, and around 125 CE it had not yet been completely finished. However, by this time it was well on the way, thanks to the efforts of their leaders and some intellectuals.

It has sometimes been argued that the Christians had achieved their autonomy over against Judaism much earlier: from the time of Jesus, from the foundation of the first church in Jerusalem, or from the time of the missionary activity of the apostle Paul. I shall show that this was not the case, and that Christianity's discovery of itself dates only from the very end of the first century CE.

So we can rightly speak of a childhood of Christianity during the three-quarters of a century which followed the death of Jesus on the cross. Certainly Christianity was born with faith in the resurrection of Christ. But just as a child only discovers itself as an autonomous person after many experiences, so the religion of Christ became aware of itself only after many events, not the least of which was the severance from Judaism which it underwent from 90 CE. Up to that time, with very rare exceptions, the Christians regarded themselves as Jews or as sympathizers with Judaism, of which there were so many around the synagogues. One can only understand their spiritual adventure and their literature of this period if one is aware of this fact.

To reconstruct a tentative progress like that of the Christians, of course we need sources. Those we have are quite abundant, but they are not as diverse as one could wish. The Judaism of the first century BCE and the first century CE is much better known to us since the discovery, half a century ago, of the Dead Sea Scrolls. This has been the occasion for a re-reading of all the inter-testamental literature that we already have. The works of Flavius Josephus and Philo of Alexandria complete our documentation on this point. But we have almost no Roman or Jewish documentation, whether literary or archaeological, which enables us to get to know Jesus and the first generations of Christians. Our only sources come from within Christian circles themselves, and that makes cross-checking difficult, all the more so since we have virtually no texts from Aramaic-speaking Christians. What we do have are mainly the writings brought together in the second century of our era to form the New Testament; to these must be added some short books and letters from the end of the first century and the beginning of the second, often grouped under the heading 'Apostolic Fathers', though this designation also covers writings later than 125. Some later texts doubtless also contain elements going back to the first Christian century (the Gospel of Thomas, the Pseudo-Clementine writings, etc.).

In total we have sufficient documentation, but it requires critical attention. That is particularly true in the case of the Christian texts. Critics often have to cast doubt on their alleged authorship, and the narrative is sometimes distorted by apologetic intentions and very marked theological tendencies. Furthermore, the dating of the various documents is difficult, and the literary relations which exist between some of them call for extremely complex analyses, for example in the case of the Gospels. These different tasks go to make up a gigantic workshop in which a very large number of specialists have been collaborating or opposing one another for at least two centuries. I shall only touch on these discussions, to avoid wearying readers and distracting them from the essentials of the account. It will be enough to make brief reference to the great critical debates and to indicate clearly which solution I favour.

There is no reason why new documents should not appear one day.

So my conclusions are provisional and are always open to modification. However, it should be noted that the ancient libraries and archaeological sites which since the middle of the last century have given us so many unpublished documents and very old manuscripts of texts known hitherto only from later copies have now been the object of very thorough investigations. So the probability of new sensational discoveries is low. The account which follows may thus be regarded as relatively trustworthy, to the degree that it interprets the available documents correctly.

Acknowledgments

The wisdom which comes with age allows an author to perceive that he has not made himself, but is the spokesman of his time and place. So it is to Strasbourg, its venerable university and the Faculty of Protestant Theology which was its initial nucleus, that I want first to express my thanks for the freedom to research and opportunities to write which they have given me now for almost half a century. It is there that this short book has matured, little by little.

My thanks also go to my wife, to whom the final form of this book owes so much. It would not have been possible without her constant support and criticism.

Christian Expansion in the First Century

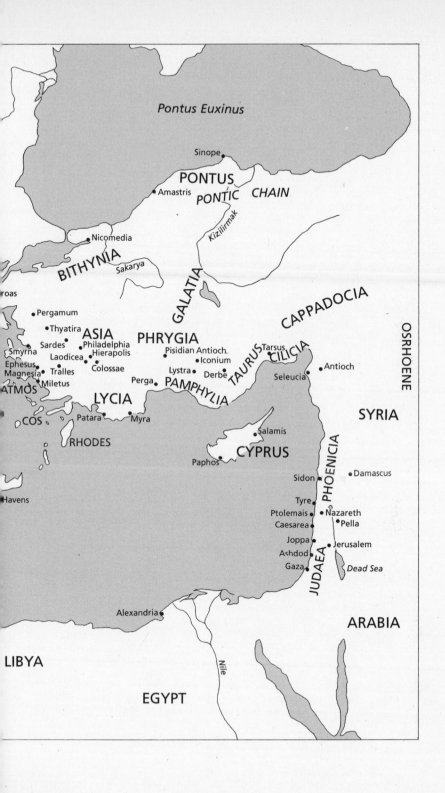

Pontus Euxinus

Sinope

PONTUS

Amastris

PONTIC CHAIN

Kizilirmak

Nicomedia

BITHYNIA

Sakarya

GALATIA

CAPPADOCIA

OSRHOENE

roas

Pergamum

Thyatira

ASIA

PHRYGIA

Sardes

Philadelphia

Smyrna

Laodicea

Hierapolis

Pisidian Antioch

Tarsus

CILICIA

Iconium

TAURUS

Ephesus

Colossae

Lystra

Derbe

Antioch

Magnesia

Tralles

Seleucia

ATMOS

Miletus

Perga

PAMPHYLIA

SYRIA

LYCIA

COS

Patara

Myra

Salamis

RHODES

CYPRUS

PHOENICIA

Damascus

Paphos

Sidon

Havens

Tyre

Ptolemais

Nazareth

Caesarea

Pella

Joppa

Jerusalem

Ashdod

JUDAEA

Gaza

Dead Sea

Alexandria

ARABIA

LIBYA

Nile

EGYPT

I

Judaism at the Beginning of Our Era

The two small kingdoms which had formed in Palestine after the reigns of David and Solomon were swept away, the first, that of Israel, by the Assyrian invasion in the eighth century BCE and the second, that of Judah, by the Babylonian invasion at the beginning of the sixth century BCE. In both cases, a large part of the surviving Jewish population was deported to Mesopotamia, where it took root. The return to Palestine made possible by the establishment of Persian domination over the whole of the Near East (at the end of the sixth century BCE) was only partial, and for long centuries Mesopotamia remained a very active centre of Jewish life. From the end of the fourth century the empire of Alexander and then the Seleucid kingdom offered the Jews who had remained in Mesopotamia opportunities for settling in Persia in the East and Syria and Anatolia in the West. At the same time, the monarchy of the Ptolemies facilitated the settling of Palestinian Jews in Egypt and in Cyrenaica. Because of this, when the Persian empire made itself master of Mesopotamia (in 170 BCE), and later when the Roman empire had annexed the whole perimeter of the eastern Mediterranean (first century BCE), these two great states found a very important Jewish Diaspora in their respective territories. It numbered several million and continued its expansion within the new political framework thus created.

This Diaspora, which for centuries had enjoyed a privileged status, had a varied but always strong local organization, as befitted a minority which wanted to keep its sense of identity. Can we speak of 'synagogues' before this time? Probably, to the degree that these institutions had a role of both teaching and jurisdiction, not to mention the task of representing the community before the local authorities. These synagogues made a marked contribution towards preserving the cohesion of the Jewish group, which they constantly reminded of the Torah. But at the same time the colonies of the Diaspora were in constant contact with the surrounding civilization, all the more so since they had adopted its languages, in particular Aramaic and Greek. The appearance of translations of the books of the Hebrew Bible into Aramaic before our era (fragmentary Targumim found at Qumran) shows that in many synagogues Hebrew was no longer understood. Similarly, the publication of a Greek translation of this collection, the Septuagint, attests that Greek had become the language used in many synagogues of the Diaspora.

These influences from the surrounding civilization were not limited to language. A certain number of philosophical or religious ideas were also welcomed in the communities of the Diaspora. Thus Platonism provided Philo of Alexandria with categories of thought, and the allegorical exegesis practised in the interpretation of Homer was applied to holy scripture by this same Philo and by other Alexandrian Jewish authors. Similarly, after undergoing the influence of Babylonian religion (the creation story, astrological themes, etc.), Mesopotamian Judaism took up a certain number of themes of Iranian religion (dualism, Last Judgment, resurrection of the dead, etc.). These can be found shortly before the Christian era at Qumran and among the Pharisees of Palestine. Furthermore, different syncretisms appeared here and there on the periphery of the synagogues: one of the most striking cases of this phenomenon is the assimilation by certain Jews of Asia Minor of the Phrygian God Sabazios to Yahweh Sabaoth, from the end of the second century BCE.

Despite all these phenomena, the Jews of the Diaspora remained faithful to their heritage, thanks to their attachment to the Jerusalem Temple. They agreed to pay a tax for this sanctuary. They zealously went on pilgrimage on the occasion of the main festivals of the Israelite calendar. Some of them had even settled in Jerusalem, in the hope of being buried there and thus having a ringside seat at the resurrection of the dead. To this was added the observance of the commandments of the Law of Moses, despite all the differences which there were in its interpretation.

Palestinian Judaism did not have the numerical importance of the Diaspora, since it did not number more than a million Jews at the beginning of the Christian era. However, unlike all the Diaspora groups, this Judaism was in the majority in its province. Palestine certainly had important minorities: the Samaritans, who occupied the centre of the province; the descendants of the Philistines, largely Hellenized, who were still living in places on the Mediterranean coast, from Raphia to Ashdod; the cities of the Decapolis, already relatively old, and the new cities (Caesarea, Bethsaida Julias, Sepphoris and Tiberias), which had a partly Jewish population but were above all populated with Syrian, Greek and Roman colonies. However, the Jews were by far the most numerous in the province, above all since the Hasmonaean dynasty had converted the population of Galilee by force (around 104–103 BCE).

Arising out of the rebellion of the Maccabees against the Hellenization imposed by Antiochus Epiphanes (166–160 BCE), this dynasty had succeeded in re-establishing an independent Jewish state in Palestine for the first time in four centuries. The series of Hasmonaean sovereigns who ruled until 37 BCE almost all exercised the function of high priest. So there seemed no objection to the integral application of the Law of Moses as the legal basis of their state. However, this demand of the pious Jews was realized only in a very partial and temporary way because of the tormented political history which Palestine experienced during this period, and the growing attraction of Hellenistic civilization for the Jews of high society. The progressive accession to power of the Herodian dynasty, which was of Idumaean origin (63–37 BCE); the reign of Herod the Great (37–4 CE); and then the establishment from 6 BCE of the direct administration of Judaea and Samaria by Rome, made this hope a vain one, even if the Jewish tribunals retained a certain autonomy.

Confronted with this painful failure, the most active circles in Palestinian Judaism adopted attitudes which can without exaggeration be called sectarian. The most privileged group was that of the Sadducees, composed of priestly families who exercised their functions in the Temple in Jerusalem. However, this very conservative group was the one that was most open to Hellenistic influences. In its eyes the regular celebration of the cult in the sanctuary chosen by God was at the centre of the Torah. So it was essential for those responsible for the Temple and its activities to maintain close relations with the political authorities, so that these respected and protected cultic life, including the pilgrimages. The other aspects of the Law were understood above all as ritual rules aimed at preserving the purity of the people for the cult. To the Sadducees, a moral and social interpretation of the commandments hardly seemed justified. Furthermore, they only partly accepted the authority of the prophetic writings, regarding only the Pentateuch as true holy scripture.

In the second century BCE a certain number of priests had seceded from this privileged group, which was satisfied with a society which did not contest its wealth based on the temple tax, in circumstances about which we know very little. Scandalized by the abuses that they saw in the life of the temple, by the compromises of the senior clergy with the most varied political authorities, and by the concessions made to the spirit of the age, over the liturgical calendar in particular, these Essenes had withdrawn into the desert, where they led an ascetic life. The discoveries at Qumran give us a more precise idea of this than we had previously. Organized into a real monastic order with rigorous discipline, and obsessed by the need to preserve their ritual purity, the Essenes refused to have anything to do with the Temple cult, which in their eyes had become illegitimate, and devoted all their efforts to meditating on the scriptures, in which they included the prophetic writings. The Teacher of Righteousness, who had founded this movement before the end of the second century BCE and had been the victim of a brutal repression, had bequeathed it a hermeneutic based on the application of the texts to the present, a passion for apocalyptic, and a theology strongly influenced by Iranian religion. Even if a kind of Essene third order seems to have existed in the main cities of Palestine, particularly in Jerusalem, such a movement was basically sectarian and isolated from the mass of the Jewish population. Its eschatological and messianic speculations were beyond their understanding and its austerity repelled them. However, its vast literary production assured it widespread influence, also in the Diaspora.

Instead of taking refuge in an impeccable ritual or in an intransigent rejection of the empirical priestly institution, like the Sadducees and Essenes, the Pharisees had opted for the transformation of an impracticable social law into a moral law which was presented to each member of the people. The Pharisees, who appeared in Palestine just before the second century BCE, only gradually gave up imposing the Law of Moses on the whole of Palestinian society. We do not know very much about their history and ideas before the destruction of the Temple, in 70 CE. However, it is clear that since they could not give the Law of Moses its eminent place in the organization of society, the Pharisees had undertaken to make the Torah a moral law offered to every Jew who was concerned to obey the divine will. They thus brought together into 'brotherhoods' those who desired to live in conformity to the Law. With this twofold aim they gave the commandments an interpretation which could be applied to the everyday life of all, and attached essential importance to the final retribution and the resurrection of the just. This great effort at moral and ritual seriousness earned them some admiration from the mass of the Jewish population of Palestine. However, it resulted in a very obvious contempt for the 'people of the land' (*Am ha-arets*), whom the Pharisees thought to be negligent in their religious and moral duties. City people like the seventeenth-century Puritans, the Pharisees scorned the peasants, whom they thought to be sunk in superstition and moral laxity. In short, they too had a sectarian attitude.

As for the Zealots, they had the same relations with the rest of the Jewish population of Palestine as any terrorist organization has with those among whom it lives. These people who, like the priest Phinehas (Numbers 25.6–13), took over from weak authorities in order to eliminate by violence those who violated the Law, sought to impose the completest observance of the commandments on the people, while making themselves popular by their acts of resistance against the Romans. We can compare them with those groups which, in Islamic countries, try to impose the *shariah* as the basis of law. Necessarily vowed to secrecy and a rigorous discipline to escape repression, they thought that they were acting for the benefit of all. However, of necessity they lived apart, in restricted circles which only rarely had contact with the mass of the people.

In short, at the beginning of the first century of our era, Palestinian Judaism was torn between minority groups inspired by the desire to give the Torah its true meaning and its true place, but in complete disagreement with one another as to how to achieve this aim, and a large majority, for the most part peasants, who lived out their adherence to the religion of Moses without bothering about particular problems. This majority practised some of the essential commandments, including the custom of going on pilgrimage to the Temple for some of the annual festivals. They avoided marriages with foreigners, but accepted with resignation a political and social order which had nothing to do with the rules of the Torah. Everyday life, with its often weighty cares, distracted these simple people from the reformist or apocalyptic dreams of zealous minority groups, who were annoyed and disturbed by so much indifference. The 'people of God' obeyed the divine will expressed in the Torah so imperfectly that there was good reason to be concerned about its future if it persisted in provoking the wrath of the Supreme Judge in this way.[1]

2

John the Baptist and Jesus of Nazareth

The inability of the minority groups to rally the mass of the Jewish people of Palestine behind them could not fail to prompt attempts to cross the barrier which separated the two. We know of two of these enterprises in the first third of the first century BCE, those of John the Baptist and Jesus.

John the Baptist is known to us only from very incomplete documents: on the one hand a passage from the *Jewish Antiquities* of the historian Flavius Josephus (XVII, 5), a work finished around 93–94 CE; on the other several passages in the New Testament. These consist of six passages common to the first three Gospels;[1] three passages common to Mark and Matthew;[2] one passage common to Matthew and Luke;[3] one passage peculiar to Matthew;[4] two passages peculiar to Luke;[5] five passages peculiar to John;[6] and seven passages peculiar to Acts.[7] These stories about John the Baptist, words attributed to him and allusions to his work are enough to attest his existence and importance, even if they leave vast twilight areas which later texts do not illuminate in any way.

This John seems to have come from a Judaean priestly family. He was born some years before our era and withdrew into the desert around 25 CE in response to a call from on high, there to lead an ascetic life. In circumstances which escape us, he acquired an extraordinary reputation and attracted considerable crowds in the desert of Judaea, to which he began to announce that God's visitation to Israel was imminent. This was a formidable prospect for a people which was neglecting its duties and thus incurring the divine wrath. So John called on his hearers to repent immediately and offered them a bath of purification in the Jordan as a pledge of the forgiveness which God guaranteed them in return. This 'baptism', as we call it, after the Greek term *baptisma*, was to be followed by reformed conduct on the part of those who had received it. Even if for some this conversion consisted in embracing the ascetic life,[8] it led the great majority of those who were attracted by John to resume their social, family and professional life with a behaviour which from then on would be exemplary.[9] All were now ready to face the last judgment with the certainty of enjoying the divine forgiveness. The spiritual breach at the heart of Israel had thus disappeared, through the grace offered by God to all. John the Baptist appeared as the prophet of the end of time, and some saw him as the Elijah *redivivus* announced by the prophet Malachi.[10]

This intrepid messenger of a God who was coming to judge his people did not hesitate to attack Herod Antipas, the son of Herod the Great to whom the Romans had granted the rule of Galilee and Peraea (from 4 BCE to 39 CE). Herod had just married his niece Herodias, previously the wife of his brother Herod Boethus (and not Philip, as the Gospels wrongly say), an action which had aroused the indignation of many Jews. John the Baptist made himself the spokesman of the opponents of this marriage, and he found such a response that the prince, disturbed at the growing popularity of this inconvenient prophet, imprisoned him in his fortress of Machaerus, in Peraea. Some time afterwards, in circumstances around which the Gospel of Mark[11] elaborates a narrative which is more picturesque than substantial, John was executed in his prison.

If we believe the Gospels, the imprisoned prophet had heard echoes of the activity of Jesus and sent a group of his followers to discover what was to be made of a form of preaching and a form of behaviour which he found sympathetic, but also disconcerting.[12] Did Jesus' reply, which paraphrases several prophecies in the book of Isaiah, convince John the Baptist that his old disciple was playing a messianic role and was turning upside down the apocalyptic scheme on which he had based his message? One can doubt it, given the silence of the Gospels about the welcome given by John to Jesus' reply. Consequently, the episodes reported by the evangelists in order to show John the Baptist paying allegiance to Jesus[13] have a legendary character. The figure whose imminent coming John the Baptist was announcing was God himself, and not a more or less human messiah. Nothing allows us to think that the baptizing prophet changed his mind, even if Jesus seemed to him to be playing a positive role.

A number of indications show that the disciples gathered by John the Baptist remained faithful to him after his death[14] and that they continued to spread his message into the Diaspora.[15] The Fourth Gospel has traces in its first chapters of a polemic which opposes the disciples of John the Baptist to those of Jesus. There John the Baptist is presented as refusing any messianic title for himself and as being a constant witness to the messiahship of Jesus, even when to do that he has to oppose his own disciples.[16] Here is evidence that towards the end of the first century CE, when this Gospel was composed, there was a community for which John the Baptist was the messiah or the prophet of the end of time. The fact that some passages relating to John the Baptist in the Gospels are visibly based on a Baptist tradition, as is the case with part of the infancy narrative of the Gospel of Luke (chs. 1–2); with the passages summarizing the preaching of John in Mark, Matthew and Luke; and with part of the prologue of the Fourth Gospel, also attests that down to the end of the first century there was at least one community which handed on this tradition. The later evidence relating to the existence of a Baptist church[17] are very scattered, but without being too rash one can see them as indications of the existence of a Baptist community on the periphery of Judaism for a good part of late antiquity. Without having experienced the development of Christianity, this community which was faithful to John the Baptist seems to have perpetuated itself in some areas of the Near East. It was almost certainly excluded from the synagogues at the time of the elimination of the *minim* at the end of the first century of our era, thus becoming a sect. This was a paradoxical end for a movement born out of a desire to bring together all the Jews in repentance to prepare for God's visitation to his people.[18]

Jesus for his part is known to us by a much more abundant documentation than is the case with John. This consists of the four Gospels of the New Testament, to which can be added several passages from the rest of this collection, and elements contained both in various apocryphal Gospels, beginning with the Gospel of Thomas which was rediscovered complete half a century ago at Nag Hammadi in Egypt, and in some patristic writings from the second and third centuries CE. However, we have no trustworthy document relating to the historical Jesus in the Jewish and pagan writings of the time, nor does archaeology give us any direct information about him or those around him. In other words, cross-checking between sources is almost impossible. Moreover, all the documents mentioned here are coloured by later Christian faith, and this makes critical investigation of the events and historical figures behind the narratives and other statements very difficult. All the material is steeped in ideas about the divinity of Christ or the mission of the church in the world.

For these reasons, for more than two centuries the study of the life of the historical Jesus has been a battlefield on which scholars have engaged in ruthless conflicts.[19] This is not the place to consider these problems at length, so I shall content myself with stating some general conclusions which seem to me to be dictated by common sense.[20]

First of all, there is no reason to doubt the historical existence of Jesus, as has sometimes been done. His figure is too well attested; he is too completely probable in his time and his setting; he is too important for explaining the sequence of events to be eliminated from history and to be made into a kind of abstract deity who was only gradually given human attributes. Secondly, however, it is clear that any reconstruction of the biography of Jesus is impossible, beyond a few basic facts. We can say with certainty that Jesus was a Palestinian Jew,[21] that he was born shortly before our era, that he lived mainly in Galilee, that he was a popular preacher and healer, and that he was executed by crucifixion in Jerusalem, around 30 CE. We can also reconstruct some of the main themes of his message and get quite a clear idea of the kind of audiences that he encountered. But we cannot claim to establish the historicity of every story and every saying; we cannot construct a chronology and a topography of his public activity with any degree of certainty; nor can we reconstruct the outer or inner course of his ministry. Once we recognize and accept these limits, we have to escape trivializing Jesus and try to grasp the meaning of his activity and his preaching.

To do that, we must first of all note that Jesus had himself baptized by John the Baptist. That is evidence of a full commitment to John's enterprise: to lead the mass of the Jewish people of Palestine to accept the promise of forgiveness offered by God on the approach of his visitation to Israel. Jesus even seems to have come from his distant Galilee to share for a while in the life of the group of John the Baptist's disciples.[22] He then parted company with them, taking with him some disciples with whom he organized his own campaign of baptisms for the crowd.[23] When John was arrested, Jesus and his group went back to Galilee and there launched on the vast undertaking of proclaiming a message which Mark calls a gospel.[24] Ceasing to baptize, they took up John's preaching while making innovations in it.

In what respects was the preaching of Jesus new by comparison with that of John the Baptist? The very profusion of the sayings of Jesus reported by the Gospels makes this question very difficult to answer, all the more so since later tradition could have distorted the meaning of what the Master said. Some elements of John's message have been retained by his old disciple: the audience continues to be the crowd, with its mixture of every social category and religious option; the proximity of God's visitation is again affirmed; the pressing call to repentance is repeated and the divine mercy remains the key to God's action towards his people. What has changed is that the imminence of the kingdom of God has been transformed into a mysterious presence;[25] the time of grace which allowed the call to repentance and the sign of baptism is now over;[26] there is no need to prepare oneself for tomorrow, because the kingdom of God must be seized today. It is somewhat difficult to understand what all this means, and it has to be admitted that some facts escape us. The kingdom of God is no longer a visible reality, but the offer of divine grace made to all when Jesus speaks and acts. It is the gathering of people before Jesus, and it is the miraculous meal which attests the presence of God among his own.[27] It is the divine power which liberates men and women by the hands of Jesus the exorcist, the healer, the conqueror of death. It is the teaching inspired by the Master, whose unique authority[28] allows him to reveal behind each commandment the unlimited demand of God,[29] and behind each human situation its profound meaning.[30]

In short, this paradoxical kingdom of God is closely bound up with the presence of Jesus among his people. Active among the little people of the countryside who had been abandoned by the organized groups,[31] ready to confront these[32] as well as the religious authorities,[33] on all the evidence Jesus is moved by a very strong sense of his mission and his relation with God. Rightly, the audacious familiarity of the address 'Abba',[34] an intimate Aramaic word for 'father', which he used as a form of address to God, has often been cited. One could also mention a saying from Matthew (26.53) which shows that Jesus felt assured of protection from on high, and one from John (2.19–20), about his certainty of being able to mobilize the divine power itself if need be.

Must we speak in this connection of a 'messianic consciousness' of Jesus, as many have done? The term is not a happy one, since the mission with which Jesus felt himself to be invested has only a distant relationship to the conceptions of the messiah which were widespread in the Judaism of his time, whether this was a political messiah or a priestly messiah. But there is no disputing the fact that Jesus had a very lofty idea of the role with which God had entrusted him for the establishment of his kingdom. Did he use the apocalyptic term Son of Man borrowed from Daniel (7.13–14) and the literature put under the pseudonym of Enoch to designate himself? This is an extremely complex problem, which we cannot investigate here. Suffice it to say that this is not impossible,[35] all the more so since in Aramaic this phrase was also a way of designating oneself without using the detestable 'I'.

Be this as it may, Jesus' extraordinary claim to be close to God, though with all the Jewish tradition he conceived God as transcendent, without doubt contributed to the catastrophe which prematurely interrupted his activity. This activity had lasted between eighteen months and three years, and had taken place mainly in Galilee. During a pilgrimage to Jerusalem, Jesus had provoked a brief scuffle around the stalls of the traders who offered to the faithful produce to be used for offerings and sacrifices.[36] The presence of these traders within the sanctuary seemed to him to be incompatible with the sacred character of the precincts. This action, performed with authority, brought its author great prestige among the crowd of pilgrims and made him a dangerous man in the eyes of the Temple authorities and the Roman forces of occupation. At the first opportunity – we do not know whether this was some days or some months after the incident in the Temple – Jesus was arrested in the suburbs of Jerusalem by the temple guard and then, after an interrogation before the Jewish authorities, was handed over to the Romans. They condemned him to die on the cross as a disturber of public order. The execution was immediate and the disciples, who had escaped arrest, dispersed and hid, overwhelmed by this tragedy which reduced to nothing the claims of Jesus and their own role in the kingdom of God. The fourfold account of these dramatic days given us by the New Testament Gospels goes back to an archetype composed in Jerusalem a few years after the events. However, this text, intended to be read during solemn celebrations with pilgrims won over to the Christian faith, is more liturgical than historical, and gives us only a very imperfect and very biassed picture of what took place during these tragic days.[37]

Still, the disaster was complete. The kingdom of God which the peasants and fishermen of Galilee and then the pilgrims who went up to Jerusalem had believed that they could see dawning had disappeared with the death of the one who had been its bearer. After the shattering of the hopes aroused by John the Baptist came the irreparable destruction of the fragile and paradoxical edifice on which Jesus had begun work with so much talent. In short, this twofold attempt to bring the great mass of Palestinian Jews back to God had not achieved any lasting result. The way was free for the mobilization of the people by the Zealots, ending in 70 CE with the destruction of the Temple, and then the taking in hand of Judaism by the scribes of the Pharisaic party who settled at Jamnia. They were the first to bring their people back under the yoke of the Law of Moses after the disaster provoked by the Zealots.

3

The First Church of Jerusalem

However, the chapter of the history of Israel opened by Jesus was not closed. The disciples of the crucified Master had taken flight, and many of them had returned to Galilee, there to resume their ordinary existence, for example fishing on Lake Tiberias.[1] Their enthusiasm had completely gone.[2] They had been deceived, and whatever their regrets, they were not disposed to allow themselves to be mobilized again.

It was then that extraordinary phenomena took place which completely changed their attitude. These were neither cosmic signs nor public events, but private phenomena, restricted to the disciples:[3] appearances of the dead man, who affirmed that he was alive beyond death and ordered them to continue his work. There is no certain account of these appearances: the Gospel of Mark does not have one; the three other Gospels do have accounts,[4] but they are mutually incompatible; the Acts of the Apostles presents its own version[5] and gives three different accounts of the appearance of the Risen Jesus to Saul/Paul of Tarsus.[6] Nowhere in his letters does Paul relate the appearance that he was granted; he contents himself with very brief allusions to it.[7]

However, there is no doubt that these 'christophanies' were the origin of belief in Jesus as messiah and of the activity of the disciples in spreading this conviction. The very ancient confession of faith quoted by Paul in I Corinthians (15.3–7) is the best evidence of this. So it is important to have some idea of what really happened shortly after the burial of Jesus.

The late and legendary character of the various accounts makes them unusable for the historian, except in the case of the appearance to Saul of Tarsus. The three versions of this seem to go back to two independent traditions, one coming from the church of Damascus and the other from the group of missionaries accompanying Paul.[8] There, in the features common to the two traditions, is a historical nucleus to which we shall return later. The absence of an old account of other appearances can easily be explained by the sacred character of an encounter with a divine being. One could claim to have encountered the risen Jesus, as Paul himself does, and attest that others had had the same experience – but not relate the event. On the other hand, a list of the appearances of the risen Christ very quickly became an essential element of the confession of faith: the formula in I Corinthians (15.3–7), already venerable in the 50s CE when Paul was evangelizing Corinth, clearly shows this. In other words, these appearances were so important in the eyes of Christians that we must not neglect them. Another fact is interesting to historians: two of the Gospels mention one or more women as the very first people to whom Jesus appeared.[9] This fact, which was not thought worth including in the confession of faith because of the inferior status of women, has a good chance of being part of the historical nucleus which is to be retained.

Finally, mention must be made of the accounts of the discovery of the empty tomb. The fourfold account of how the women found the tomb where Jesus had been buried open and empty[10] has often been considered purely legendary. The empty tomb is not mentioned in the confession of faith in I Corinthians (15.3–7) or in the letters of Paul, which often allude to the resurrection of Christ; the presence of angels in the tomb is a mythological feature; there are important differences between the four accounts, which are all based on the idea that the tomb of Jesus was clearly identified, whereas criminals who had been executed were usually buried in a common ditch. Despite the force of these arguments, caution is called for, since the account of the empty tomb is the conclusion to a liturgical account of the passion which can be said without hesitation to have been composed in the ten years following the execution of Jesus, and moreover in Jerusalem. Given all this, the historian must certainly accept that there is a historical nucleus in this episode, which has been emphasized by substituting the testimony of the angels for the testimony of the women, since that was thought to be too fragile.[11]

So we may suppose that the discovery of the empty tomb by women who followed Jesus was followed by appearances of the Risen Christ, some granted to individuals, like Peter[12] and James,[13] and others to larger or smaller groups, like the Twelve[14] or the apostles,[15] and even to a whole gathering.[16] These appearances certainly took place in different places, some in Jerusalem, as the Gospel of Luke and John 20 affirm, and others in Galilee[17] or elsewhere.[18] As for their date, we can only say that they began shortly after the discovery of the empty tomb and that they lasted several months, perhaps several years, despite the effort made by the author of the Acts of the Apostles to limit them to the forty days following the resurrection.[19]

We know nothing of the reactions, the confabulations, perhaps the polemic, prompted by these earth-shaking events. At most we can say that to judge from the construction of the confession of faith quoted by Paul in I Corinthians (15.3–7), the appearances involved two groups, one associated with Peter, who was one of the very first disciples of Jesus, i.e. the Twelve, and a community of more than five hundred brethren, and the other associated with James, brother of the Lord, i.e. 'all the apostles'. This bipolarity of the groups involved in the christophanies is a brute fact which our documentation does not allow us to analyse more closely. We can only say that the group around Peter has the look of a religious community with a framework deriving its authority from the close relations which it had had with Jesus during his public ministry, whereas James seems to enjoy a dynastic legitimacy which authorizes him to delegate his authority to representatives – since according to the Jewish usage of the term, that is the meaning of the word 'apostle'. If we are to believe Acts[20] and Galatians,[21] these two figures and their followers could soon be found side by side in Jerusalem, where they had decided to settle.

That was a surprising choice. Instead of profiting from the sympathy aroused by the activity of Jesus in Galilee, a region moreover from which they had originally come, those who witnessed the appearances of the Risen Christ rushed into the lion's mouth, to the place where the Temple authorities and the Roman authorities had collaborated in getting rid of Jesus. This paradoxical choice can be understood only if we accepted a twofold motivation on the part of the members of the two groups. Persuaded first of all that the Temple and the Holy City were the place chosen by God for his eschatological intervention, they evidently thought that Christ, whose resurrection demonstrated his legitimacy, would return there to finish his work which had been tragically interrupted. So it was fitting for the faithful followers of the Risen Christ to be there to welcome their Master on his return. That was worth accepting some risks for.

Moreover, those who had received appearances of the Risen Christ had all understood this overwhelming event as a mission command. They felt that from then on they had been mandated to continue the preaching of their Master to Israel. However, by reason of the circumstances, the affirmation of the presence of the kingdom of God associated with the person of Jesus was transformed into an announcement of the imminence of Christ's return on earth, which would soon bring about this divine kingdom that was so eagerly awaited. What better place to spread this message than the city to which the pilgrims flocked *en masse* several times a year, coming from all Jewish Palestine and the Diaspora?

Doubtless some of the supporters of Jesus remained in the villages of Galilee where they had met the Master. We shall find them there later. But there is no justification for claiming that they were organized into religious communities distinct from the synagogues. Doubtless they continued in their jobs and their family life, while gratefully cherishing the memory of what Jesus had brought them. They were fertile ground for the later activity of Christian preachers rather than a group capable of enunciating a distinctive theology or christology.

The situation of the groups established in Jerusalem was quite different. The Acts of the Apostles gives us a mass of more or less solid information about them, particularly in chapters 1–5. So we need to pay critical attention to these chapters in order to arrive at a probable reconstruction of the institutions, the life and the thought of this nucleus of a few dozen people, soon enlarged by the adherence of a substantial number of brethren who were won over by the preaching of the spokesmen of the Risen Christ.

The initial nucleus mentioned in Acts (1.13–15) was made up of the disciples and relatives of Jesus who had come from Galilee. To finance their settlement in Jerusalem they seem to have sold their properties and put the money realized from the sales into a common fund. Some at least of the brothers who joined them in the capital did the same thing, and in return for this sacrifice were admitted into the group of the 'saints'.[22] The prestige of that group was sufficiently great to prompt fraudulent manoeuvres on the part of unscrupulous candidates, as is shown by the sorry story of Ananias and Sapphira.[23] The administration of the common fund was guaranteed by the 'Twelve', a group of disciples apparently designated by Jesus during his lifetime.[24] As I remarked earlier, they received the first appearances of the Risen Christ after their driving force, Simon who was called 'Peter'. Leaving aside the probable reference to the twelve tribes of Israel,[25] the leadership role of the 'Twelve' bears a striking resemblance to the authority attributed at Qumran to a group of 'twelve men and three priests'.[26] Perhaps here we have an indication of Essene influence on the first church in Jerusalem. Its practice of having communal possessions could also be inspired by the Qumran model, even if the original motive behind it had been empirical.

It might perhaps be objected that as far as we know, Jesus had had no contact with Essenism and that a religious group which had come to establish itself in the holy city did not have much in common with these coenobites in the desert of Judaea. Indeed, but the disciples of Jesus, deprived of the presence of their master, had to re-invent everything, and the Essenes offered them both reflection on the messiah and an interpretation of the prophecies which brought their content up to date, not to mention an attractive institutional model. It has to be added that an Essene third order seems to have been set up in certain places in Palestine, including Jerusalem, where archaeology has uncovered the existence of an Essene quarter. In short, the existence of relations between the Essenes and the first disciples of Jesus gathered together at Jerusalem is by no means out of the question – quite the contrary. But it would be naive to believe that the Christian community was merely a copy of Essenism. However, it would be even more naive to believe that the church took shape without being subject to the influence of this great Jewish anti-establishment movement.[27]

As I have already said, the Essene model was largely imitated by the first church on an institutional level: a central group of 'saints' who enjoyed great authority, around a collective of twelve men who held all the power; the sharing of goods within this nucleus; rigorous discipline imposed on members of the group; very widespread solidarity between the members of this group, but also with all members in need, beginning with the widows.[28] The whole community, and even more the central nucleus, led a very active and very organized liturgical life. At the hours of Jewish prayer, its members gathered in the portico of the Temple,[29] where their presence aroused both a degree of popular enthusiasm and more or less lively reactions from the priestly authorities. The everyday practice of communal meals with liturgical elements about which we know virtually nothing was reserved for the more private meetings which brought the brethren together in one another's homes.[30] We know nothing of the conditions on which baptism was administered; it seems to have been practised very early,[31] and must have been a rite of admission closely resembling the baptism of John the Baptist. Teaching was given in the house meetings, in particular by the Twelve.[32] This certainly included a christological interpretation of the person and work of Jesus, accompanied by references to scripture and moral exhortations.

In addition to this everyday liturgical life, there was a celebration of the festivals of the calendar, as was natural in a Jewish setting, beginning with shabbat. However, it seems that from the start the disciples of Jesus added new liturgical actions to the Jewish rites, not all of which they celebrated, above all when they involved bloody sacrifices. The evening after the sabbath, or the next morning, they celebrated the resurrection of Jesus Christ in their homes, perhaps on the basis of lists of appearances like that in I Corinthians 15. That is the origin of the practice of Sunday worship. During the festivals which drew crowds of pilgrims to Jerusalem, especially at the time of Passover, the passion of Jesus was commemorated in a more public way. The brethren in Jerusalem joined those who had come to the capital as pilgrims at the places of some of the episodes which had marked the last days of the Master; here the stages of his martyrdom were recited to them. This is the origin of the accounts of the passion given by the four Gospels, which all go back to the same archetype. This archetype may be said to have acquired its definitive form less than ten years after these tragic events. The privileged place occupied in this long narrative by the account of Jesus' last supper with his disciples suggests that these gatherings included a commemorative meal which was more solemn than the everyday community meals. In short, what subsequently came to be called the eucharist was added to what in the second and third centuries were called *agapai*.

The leaders of the community did not only engage in activities relating to its government, discipline and liturgy. Their essential task was to provide its members with a teaching which was capable of giving a positive sense to the tragic events which had snatched their Master away from them, and to the life of the community and of each of the brethren. Holy Scripture offered some keys towards understanding the paradoxical destiny of Jesus, wherever it spoke of the suffering of the Righteous One or the Servant of the Lord, all the more so since these passages almost always ended in an affirmation of the divine triumph and the return to life of the unfortunate oppressed. Like the Essenes, the first Christians regarded these ancient texts as prophecies about events which had taken place before their eyes and saw in them above all the proclamation of the death and resurrection of Jesus and the affirmation of their saving character. Some other passages about the divine forgiveness, the outpouring of the Holy Spirit and the love of the brethren were applied to the first church and its members, just as the Qumran people had read their own destiny in them. Do we have to follow the English critic C.H.Dodd[33] in thinking that in fact the first Christians reduced Holy Scripture to around forty chapters in which they read such prophecies? Do we even have to think that the Bible of the first Christians consisted only of a few verses prophesying the fate of Jesus and the first disciples, as has also been argued? That would be to go too far. But there were certainly degrees in the authority attributed to the holy books, which we may be sure were not read as wholes.

Another source of the teaching lavished by the first Christian teachers was the rich treasure of messianic titles developed by the Essenes from elements provided by Holy Scripture. Titles given to the Teacher of Righteousness or one of the messiahs of the end of time were transferred *en masse* to Jesus: Messiah, translated 'Christ' in Greek; Prophet, often with reference to Deuteronomy 18.15, 18–19; Lord, a title reserved for God in the Jewish Bible; Servant of God; the Holy and the Righteous One; Prince and Saviour, etc. There is no point in looking for any order or developed doctrine in this profusion. What emerges clearly is a desire to make Jesus the last messenger from God to humankind, the bearer of perfect revelation and total redemption. It is not too much to say that the first church of Jerusalem created christology, and that Christian thought was built on this basis.

The teaching given by the leaders of the first church to its faithful also had a large moral element. For them the Mosaic Law remained an essential point of reference in this area, as was the case with all the Jews. But this was the law as Jesus had interpreted it, stamped with the twofold commandment of love of God and love of neighbour;[34] a quest behind the commandments – in particular those of the Decalogue – for the unlimited demand of God;[35] a universalization of the still somewhat tribal notion of 'neighbour',[36] and so on. Understood in this way, the Law became an appeal directed to the individual conscience rather than a rule regulating social life. To make this transformation indisputable, the teaching of the Master, already memorized in his lifetime, was preserved with great care and transmitted to the new converts. This tradition, originally entirely oral, was gradually put into shape, and it assumed written form. In addition to the sayings of Jesus about the significance of the Law it also included stories of the controversies in which the Master was involved when confronted with various adversaries, and various sayings relating to the end of time, the kingdom of God, the relationship between Jesus and the Father, and some parables illustrating this teaching. This teaching, together with various additions to which we shall return, forms the basis of the first three canonical Gospels.[37]

The community, organized and taught in this way, did not live apart from the world. By choosing to live in a city – and moreover a city which was a pilgrimage centre – it had opted for close relations with the surrounding society. These relations were dominated by the efforts to spread the gospel which characterized this group and above all its leaders. By visiting the Temple regularly and seizing every occasion for evangelizing the crowd, the first Christians certainly provoked opposition, but at the same time they gained numerous followers. The account in Acts 3–5 gives us a picture of this; it is coloured by legend, but in essentials is quite faithful. Even if we need to be cautious about the impressive numbers given in Acts,[38] it seems that the several dozen people who came from Galilee rapidly won over a certain number of their compatriots to their cause. The great gatherings of pilgrims for the spring and autumn festivals were also particularly favourable occasions for spreading the good news of the imminence of the kingdom of God, which Jesus was to usher in. Since the pilgrims came both from the Diaspora and from Palestinian Judaism, we can accept that the gospel thus spread widely. Some communities could have come into existence in this way, for example in Damascus, Joppa and Lydia,[39] without the preachers in Jerusalem having to travel at all. However, the leaders of the first church took account of these small communities outside Jerusalem and adopted the habit of going to support them and to remind them that the mother community in the Holy City was the seat of spiritual authority.

This authority was indicated by the name given to the Christian assembly in Jerusalem. The Greek form of this name, *ekklesia*, denotes the general assembly of a city and thus at first sight does not have any religious significance. However, the Greek version of the Hebrew Bible called the Septuagint uses this term to translate the Hebrew phrase *qehal Yahweh*, which denotes the general assembly of the people in the wilderness, convened by Moses. In short, in a Jewish milieu *ekklesia tou theou* denoted the gathering of the chosen people. By using this term, whether in its Hebrew, Aramaic or Greek form, the Jerusalem community was presenting itself as something quite different from a simple religious movement: it was affirming itself as the prefiguration of the assembly of all the chosen people before its God. The groups outside Jerusalem[40] belonged to the same 'church' and were under the same authorities, who could visit them to make certain that everything there was taking place according to the rules.

While the audience which received the preaching of the gospel was entirely made up of Jews, it had great cultural diversity. Despite its legendary form, the account of Pentecost given in Acts 2 attests that even outside the pilgrimages, Jerusalem attracted Jews from the most distant Diaspora, who settled there in order to be near to the sanctuary. Once they had been won over to the Christian faith, these people could play a very active role in preaching to their compatriots who had come as pilgrims.

We are rather better informed about one of these groups of non-Palestinian Jews who had settled in Jerusalem and were receptive to the Christian preaching: the one which the Acts of the Apostles calls, very generally, 'Hellenists'. This group seems to have made different doctrinal choices from those of the majority. With the backing of the Twelve, it gave itself a group of seven leaders all of whom had Greek names but all of whom, with the exception of a proselyte, were Jews. According to Acts (6.3ff.), this new group had the responsibility of 'serving tables', while the Twelve retained the functions of preaching and prayer. However, those of the Seven about whom we learn something later are above all missionaries, both preachers and miracle workers.[41] One could therefore suppose that the arrangement between the Twelve and the Seven evoked in Acts does not correspond to reality. The Seven were in fact created to perform for the Hellenists the role that the Twelve performed for the whole of the first community. So this was a schism, even if it came about by mutual consent.

To get to that point there had to have been more than a difference in language and clashes over the distribution of social welfare to the widows. It is extremely probable that there were doctrinal differences and different attitudes towards the surrounding milieu.[42] The aggressiveness of Stephen, the chief spokesman of the Hellenists, about the Temple[43] is a complete break with the attitude of the Twelve, who led the community to pray in the sanctuary. Whereas the majority of the first church adopted a somewhat conciliatory attitude towards the Temple authorities, even if they did not go so far as to take part in sacrificial worship, Stephen and his followers sought a confrontation with these authorities, whom they saw as real idolaters. In fact the conflict seems to have broken out very soon after the emancipation of the Seven, which itself came shortly after the foundation of the first church. In short, beyond question, after no more than one or two years, the security of the first Christians was put in danger by the verbal excesses of some of the Hellenists. The lynching of Stephen[44] sparked off a crisis with the Jewish authorities, though they made a distinction between the Twelve, who were ardent but conciliatory, and those who followed the views of the Seven, who were much more disruptive.[45] These latter were forced to flee Jerusalem and Judaea in order to escape the authority of the Sanhedrin in the capital. Doubtless the members of the community who remained close to the Twelve could remain in the Holy City, where they continued to be tolerated.

Thus rid of this dissident group, the church in Jerusalem was nevertheless not completely united. A much less vocal group than that of the Hellenists had formed around a disciple of Jesus, perhaps John, one of the Twelve, in circumstances unknown to us. The most certain indication of the existence of such a group is the presence behind the Fourth Gospel of a particular tradition of the actions and words of Jesus, related at some points to the tradition conveyed by the circles around the Twelve but at the same time original and firmly rooted in Palestinian soil. Apparently, what has been called the 'Johannine circle' was more Judaean than the primitive nucleus of the great church, where the Galileans were in a majority. Perhaps it led a separate existence as a community and also had links with priestly circles;[46] that would explain some of the characteristics underlying the Fourth Gospel. However, this marginal group does not seem ever to have broken with the majority of the church. Consequently the two currents of the tradition have much in common, in particular the account of the Passion, which is very close in the Fourth Gospel to the version of it given by the first three Gospels. The basic difference between these two currents is rather of a theological order. The concentration on the person of Christ is much stronger in the Johannine tradition, and this tendency would only be accentuated in the redaction of the Gospels.[47]

The primitive community in Jerusalem, which was expanding very rapidly, criss-crossed by divergent currents and much influenced by an Essenism which was vigorously opposed to priestly circles, could not for very long enjoy the almost ideal stability attributed to it by the first chapters of the Acts of the Apostles. Despite the extreme discretion of this work, we can guess that the harmonious community of the first years did not succeed in surviving for long. Perhaps the crisis sparked off by the persecution of Herod Agrippa, which can be dated precisely to the first months of 44 CE, merely precipitated a development which had already begun. But it marks the transition from the primitive community to a church life more closely resembling what would subsequently be the ordinary regime of this institution.

King Herod Agrippa, grandson of Herod the Great, succeeded after 41 in reunifying the Jewish lands of Palestine under his rule, with the help of Rome. He relied on the support of priestly circles, who recognized his contribution towards averting the threat of the erection of an imperial statue in the temple, which was at one time envisaged by Caligula. It was probably on their instigation that he had James, brother of John and one of the Twelve, beheaded; however, we do not know the immediate cause of this execution.[48] Since it met with public approval, Herod Agrippa had Peter arrested shortly before Passover 44 and prepared his trial for after the festival.[49] Before an appearance in court which could have threatened the whole church, Peter escaped in fantastic circumstances which the author of Acts presents as a divine intervention.[50] He had no alternative but to flee in order to escape the royal police, and this he did without delay, after telling some brethren to warn James, the brother of the Lord.[51] Peter had saved his head, but not his authority. In fact, despite the extreme reticence of the author of the Acts of the Apostles, it is clear that from then on Peter ceased to exercise supreme authority in the Jerusalem church. He only reappears there as a missionary to the pagans, at a meeting devoted to the problems posed by the evangelization of non-Jews.[52] His status sank from being that of an inspired leader endowed with a quasi-divine authority to that of a more or less itinerant evangelist, whose word no longer had sufficient authority among the Jerusalem brethren to conclude a fundamental debate.[53]

The authority which he thus lost passed to James, brother of the Lord, as is suggested by Acts 12.17 and demonstrated by Acts 15.13–21. James had the task of drawing conclusions from the debate on the evangelization of the pagans and putting forward a solution which would commend itself to all. During Paul's last visit to Jerusalem, between ten and twelve years later, James is presented as the chief leader of the church,[54] though the Acts of the Apostles does its best not to speak of this figure whose choices were alien to it. The importance of James' role also emerges from the mentions made of him by Paul, his chief adversary, in his letters. As I remarked earlier, James is mentioned among the first to whom the risen Christ appeared according to I Corinthians (15.7), a very old confessional text which Paul cites here. Furthermore, Paul claims that on his first visit to Jerusalem, the only person whom he met other than Peter, whom he had come to see, was James, whom he expressly calls 'the brother of the Lord'.[55] So from that moment, which we must put around the middle of the 30s CE, James was an important figure in the church of the Holy City, though Peter was still its unchallenged leader. By the time of Paul's second visit to the church of the capital, apparently eleven years later,[56] James has incontestably become the head of the church, whom Peter and John help in the evangelization of the Jews.[57] Some time later James displays the features of a formidable leader, whose authority extends to all the Christian communities of the Diaspora and is imposed even on Peter.[58] In short, from 44 CE, someone who was still only a respected figure became the pope of the Jerusalem church and, by the same token, of the universal church.[59]

This fact is confirmed by various later traditions whose value would seem unquestionable.[60] As has been said numerous times for eighty years now, the authority of James in the church, which was based on that of the 'brothers of the Lord',[61] has an undoubted dynastic colouring, like the caliphate in Islam. The emphasis on the Davidic descent of Jesus, which we see developing on various sides,[62] is surely not unconnected with this tendency. Moreover, James' successor as head of the Jerusalem church was a certain Symeon, first cousin of Jesus;[63] and two grandsons of Jude, Jesus' brother, seem to have played an important role in the church in the reign of Domitian.[64] Even if these facts are not at all well known, they serve as confirmation of the existence of a dynastic current in the Palestinian Christianity of the first century. Moreover this current provoked resistance which expressed itself in the questioning of the Davidic origin of Jesus[65] and in the unbelief attributed to the whole of his family, or more precisely to his brothers,[66] at least during the lifetime of Jesus.

In short James, brother of the Lord, enjoyed a particularly marked legitimacy which derived from his kinship with Jesus. So with the help of a new leading group, that of the 'elders',[67] he was able to take the Jerusalem church in hand over a long period and through it the universal church. While still in its beginnings, this was developing rapidly. The only text to give us an idea of James as a person is that in which Eusebius relates his martyrdom.[68] A rigorous ascetic, who observed the Mosaic law very strictly, he prayed assiduously in the Temple and was regarded by the people as a powerful intercessor. So the Jewish leaders were jealous of his popularity, which made him a rival of the high priest. This note contains many legendary features, but it certainly should not be dismissed entirely. At all events it shows that James, a great preacher of the Messiah Jesus, remained a Jew who observed the law impeccably. The few passages of the New Testament which mention him attribute a relatively open attitude to him: he accepted compromises for converts of pagan origin[69] in order to encourage their evangelization.[70]

Doubtless this tendency to compromise in tricky situations was also part of the way in which James governed the Jerusalem church. The rigidity of the institutions established in the first year seems to have been loosened. The very strict communal discipline seems to have been relaxed, while the sharing of possessions disappeared, to be replaced by intensive charitable activity. Here contributions from outside were welcome,[71] perhaps because the 'poor' had a prominent place in the social composition of the church. In short, the Essene influence of the beginnings had retreated in the face of that of the Pharisaic brotherhoods.

However, on one point the orientation given by James to the Jerusalem church remained rigid, despite the sense of compromise which was introduced at first. The authority of Jerusalem was exercised with vigilance in the life of the Christian communities of Palestine and of the Diaspora. Centrifugal tendencies were manifesting themselves in these communities and endangering the cohesion of the Christian movement (communities in Palestine and Syria founded by the Hellenists, Paul's personal missionary enterprise). James and his followers vigorously tried to defend the unity that they felt to be threatened. Barnabas was sent to Antioch in Syria to avoid any drift due to the success of the preaching of the gospel to Greeks;[72] various Jerusalem prophets followed him somewhat later and there called into being a movement of solidarity towards the 'brethren living in Judaea'.[73] This was a good way of reinforcing the still fragile links between Christians in remote regions. The Jerusalem meeting made it possible to arrive at a reasonable compromise on the question of converts of pagan origin, and two envoys of the mother church, Jude and Silas, went to Antioch to communicate this agreement and strengthen the faith of the brethren there.[74] A little later, when Peter was in Antioch, much to Paul's indignation[75] 'people from James' stopped the eucharistic meals shared by Jewish Christians, including Peter and Barnabas, and Christians of pagan origin.[76] Paul was subsequently obliged to counter opponents who followed in his footsteps in all the cities in which he had preached, reminding the converts of the need to stay in line with the Jewish Law if they wanted to remain in communion with the Jerusalem church.[77] It has sometimes been argued that these Judaizers had nothing to do with Jerusalem and with James. One fact that makes this thesis highly improbable is that when Paul had become convinced that there was no longer any place for him in the East,[78] he thought that he could not avoid going to Jerusalem to offer the church there a collection made in the churches which he had founded, before setting off for Rome and Spain,[79] even though he feared that this collection would not be accepted. Thus Paul showed that he was well aware of the source of the opposition that he encountered everywhere. In order to be rid of it, so that he could evangelize Spain with the support of the Roman Christians, he wanted to be reconciled with James and the leading group in the Jerusalem church by showing them that he did not reject the unity to which in their eyes he was a serious threat.

The account given by the Acts of the Apostles of Paul's journey to Jerusalem at the head of a large delegation from the churches around the Aegean Sea[80] shows, despite its eirenic character, that the welcome given to Paul and the other leaders of the mother church was extremely reserved. He was treated as an importunate visitor whose arrival endangered the internal peace of the church in the capital. He was forced to undergo a humiliating purification in the temple. And when he had been arrested by the Romans after being threatened with lynching by the Jewish crowd, the church did not lift a finger to help him. Paul had challenged the authority of James too long for anyone to take the risk of showing the least solidarity with him, even when he had come to make his surrender. We can judge from this intransigence the degree to which the head of the Jerusalem church regarded himself as the universal bishop.

Personally prone to compromise, as we have seen, James was thus led by his conception of a Christian unity based on continued observance of the Law to reject any slackening of the minimal rules imposed by the Jerusalem church on converts of pagan origin shortly after the meeting in 48. But these rules had been conceived to facilitate the life of a non-Jewish minority within communities in which the majority were Jews. As soon as the number of Christians of pagan origin became too great, to the point where they were in the majority, the observance of these rules became precarious, even where, they were not felt, as in the churches founded by Paul, to be completely outmoded. Hence the incident in Antioch.[81] This was the evident consequence of a change in the majority, resulting in a situation which had convinced Peter and

Barnabas that the Jerusalem rule was outdated, until the day when those sent by James had reminded them of the rule made by the mother church. It is above all because of James' action that in the second century CE the four prohibitions stated in Acts (15.20–29) seem to have been the law of all the churches, though initially they only related to those in Syria and Cilicia.[82] However, these prohibitions, which were ritual in origin (respect for the Mosaic laws on killing animals in the case of the first three, and respect for Mosaic legislation on marriage for the last), were increasingly interpreted as moral commandments in a church context in which the Jews were only a tiny minority. They were seen as prohibitions against taking part in pagan sacrifice, against homicide and sexual misconduct, and as a call to observe the Golden Rule (which replaces the prohibition against eating the meat of animals which have been strangled).[83]

The long period during which the Jerusalem church flourished and influenced all the Christian communities outside the Holy City was to come to a brutal end, with the martyrdom of James and with the catastrophe which struck the Jewish capital and its temple shortly afterwards. We have two very different accounts of the first of these events, one from Flavius Josephus[84] and one from Eusebius,[85] who reproduces a fragment of the *Memoirs* of Hegesippus, a Palestinian author from the second half of the second century. Even if the Josephus passage has been retouched by a later Christian hand, it remains by far the earlier and is to be preferred. It puts in 62 CE the death by stoning of James and 'some others', after they had been condemned by the Sanhedrin of Jerusalem on the instigation of the high priest Hanan, who had taken advantage of an interval between Roman prefects to convene this assembly. The charge levelled against the accused was that they had violated the Mosaic law, but public opinion in Jerusalem does not seem to have accepted that the condemned men were guilty. Hegesippus' account puts the death of James closer to the beginning of the siege of Jerusalem by the Romans in 69 and makes it a lynching by a group of 'scribes and Pharisees', disturbed at the success of his preaching. We should simply note that it was the Jewish leaders of Jerusalem who eliminated a trouble-maker.[86] Be this as it may, the blow seems to have been a harsh one for the Jerusalem church which, even had it not been unsettled after the death of its leader, could only have succeeded in finding a successor to him after the destruction of the temple in 70.[87] Eusebius reports that when the Roman army besieged the capital, on which the Zealots had imposed a rule of terror, the Christians fled to

Pella, a pagan city of the Decapolis east of the Jordan.[88] Various historians have cast doubt on this fact, but we must probably accept that it is well founded.[89] At most we might assume that, deprived of the leader who had guided it for so long, the community dispersed, leaving some of its members who had joined the Zealots in the capital, while its leaders settled in Pella, and other of the faithful took refuge far from the combat zones. At all events, even if the church returned to Jerusalem after 70, the influence that it had exercised over all the communities outside the capital in the time of Peter and James was not re-established. The very centralized regime which had existed before 62 gave way to a complete congregationalism. This favoured dispersion at the very moment when Judaism was re-establishing in Jamnia a powerful centre which was going to undertake a reform and offer all the synagogues what we have to call an orthodoxy.

4

The Spread of the 'Hellenists'

The Greek-speaking Christian Jews who had been forced to flee Jerusalem before the middle of the 30s CE by the crisis connected with the lynching of Stephen[1] were not content with taking shelter from the threat posed by the Sanhedrin of the capital. Wherever they went, they resumed their activity as intransigent preachers of the messiahship of Jesus.[2] Some stories in the Acts of the Apostles are the only documents which inform us about this. In chapter 8 it is Philip, the second of the Seven,[3] who is at the centre of the two episodes related. The first takes place in 'the city of Samaria',[4] an ambiguous phrase which some manuscripts have tried to correct to 'a city of Samaria', without improving things much. Beyond question the author means the capital of Samaria, i.e. the city of the same name, which was destroyed in 108 BCE by the Jewish king Hyrcanus I, but which Pompey and then Herod the Great had rebuilt under the name of Sebaste. However, the location of the scenes which follow remains somewhat uncertain.

Philip's preaching in this city was accompanied by 'signs', comprising exorcisms and marvellous healings,[5] which caused great joy in the city.[6] It was a great success[7] and led to the baptism of both women and men.[8] A certain Simon had already enjoyed even greater success in this city by practising a quite comparable activity, even if the author of Acts speaks in a clearly malicious way of magic and claims to greatness[9] in this connection. In the eyes of his numerous admirers, Simon was 'the power of God which is called great';[10] this amounts both to a recognition of the divine and not satanic origin of his power and the affirmation of a close relation with God.

Despite these extraordinary pretensions, Simon was so impressed – the author of Acts tells us – by Philip's preaching 'of the kingdom of God and the name of Jesus Christ' that he too was converted, had himself baptized and followed Philip, whose 'signs and great miracles' astounded him.[11] This discipleship is presented as sincere, and gives the reader the impression that the superiority of Jesus Christ impressed itself on Simon through Philip's missionary activity.

The sequel to the story, which seems to come from another tradition and certainly reflects the personal convictions of the author of Acts, questions this positive evaluation of Philip's ministry. Peter and John, sent by the church of Jerusalem, hear in Samaria the news that this region had 'received the word of God'.[12] They immediately note a serious defect in Philip's work: those baptized have not received the Holy Spirit, although baptism has been administered to them 'in the name of the Lord Jesus'.[13] The two envoys from Jerusalem remedy this deficiency (8.17) by the laying on of hands. Does that mean that Philip had a conception of Christian baptism different from that of the church of Jerusalem? We may note that, in the next story,[14] the baptism of the Ethiopian eunuch is not associated with the gift of the Holy Spirit either;[15] the Spirit only makes an appearance to transport Philip immediately after the ceremony. The difference between Philip and the mother church is that he feels free to baptize non-Jews who have not received the Holy Spirit, whereas in the eyes of Peter and his associates only the gift of the Spirit to non-Jews authorizes the missionary to give them baptism, which is normally reserved for Jews.[16] In short, Peter and John consider that Philip has been lax, which doubtless explains why they do not even make contact with him during this episode.

The sequel to the story[17] confirms what the people from Jerusalem see as Philip's irresponsibility. He has baptized Simon the magician and accepted him as a permanent companion. Now Simon has been so badly converted that he thinks that he can buy from the apostles the power to give the Holy Spirit by the imposition of hands. Peter rebukes him in no uncertain terms and casts doubt on the authenticity of his faith. Here is another black mark against Philip, who is after all only a mediocre missionary.

With the account of the conversion of the Ethiopian eunuch[18] we return to a tradition which is much more favourable to Philip. He is seen as God's obedient instrument for evangelizing someone who was on the periphery of Judaism, since his mutilation prevented him from joining the people of God, despite his exemplary piety, which had led him to Jerusalem to worship God there. This unusual and transient encounter is organized by a divine intervention and ends up with the baptism of the foreign nobleman. Here, too, there is no question of the gift of the Holy Spirit; this confirms how liberal the Hellenist missionary is over the admission of non-Jews to the fraternity of the baptized. Moreover this story presents Philip as an inspired figure who has some similarities to the prophet Elijah.[19] Finally, it is striking that Acts 8.32–35 is the only passage in the New Testament in which the text of Isaiah 53 about the Servant of the Lord is applied to Jesus and his unjust death. Could it be that the idea of the vicarious suffering of Christ was an idea which was particularly dear to the Hellenists?

After his miraculous transportation in v.39, Philip found himself in Ashdod, one of the coastal cities of Palestine, which he evangelized before going north, preaching from city to city until he reached the Roman capital of the province, Caesarea. There he settled.[20] The population of all these places had a non-Jewish majority, so they escaped the jurisdiction of the Jerusalem Sanhedrin. It seems that Philip founded communities in them which Peter came to visit shortly afterwards, in order to link them to Jerusalem.[21] However, he did not make contact with their founder. Some twenty years later Philip was still at Caesarea, in an atmosphere charged with prophecy;[22] he had little to do with the Jerusalem church.[23] We might suppose that the person whom Acts 21.8 calls 'Philip the evangelist' had meanwhile continued his missionary enterprise from his base in Caesarea, near to Samaria, the Decapolis and Galilee, where the activity of Jesus had certainly left its mark.

Other 'Hellenists' driven from Jerusalem by the persecution following the martyrdom of Stephen had taken the gospel as far as Phoenicia, Cyprus and Antioch in Syria.[24] We do not know their identity, nor the details of their missionary enterprise, which was aimed at the synagogues of these maritime provinces. On the other hand we do know that it was at Antioch, a great cosmopolitan city, that evangelization went beyond the bounds of the synagogue. Preachers from Cyprus and Cyrenaica proclaimed 'the Lord Jesus' there to Greeks, or at least to people living in the Greek style,[25] and were very successful. The Jerusalem church got wind of this episode and sent one of its Cypriot members, the Levite Barnabas, to check that this was not a dangerous development. Barnabas gave his approval to what was going on in Antioch and settled there, at the same time becoming one of the authorities in the local community.[26] This produced a kind of fusion between the 'Hellenist' mission and the delegates from the Jerusalem church, since after a while Barnabas joined up with a certain Saul of Tarsus, a Jew from Cilicia, whom he had himself introduced to the leading group of the Jerusalem church some years earlier.[27] We shall have to discuss this unusual figure again in due course. The other eminent members of the community in Antioch[28] were doubtless 'Hellenist' preachers. Symeon called Niger and Lucius of Cyrene, who had Latin names or surnames, and Manaen, a childhood friend of Herod Antipas, all give the impression of being Jews at ease in the Roman empire.

The mixed community thus formed in the great city of northern Syria displayed interesting characteristics. The author of Acts first of all[29] notes that it was at Antioch that the disciples were first called *christianoi* (Christians), a political term, formed with the Latin ending -*ianus* and denoting 'the supporters of the Anointed One (of God)'. This term could have been ironic, since to people without any biblical background it would have suggested a group of 'supporters of the oiled one'. As often in history, it could have been adopted proudly by those concerned and given an entirely positive sense by them. In that case, here we would have an indication of a first contact with pagan circles. Furthermore, the author of Acts calls the Antiochene community the *ekklesia*,[30] a term hitherto reserved for the Jerusalem church and encompassing the communities which were created by its action. This is a sign of the emancipation of the Christian assembly of Antioch from the mother church. Do we have to attribute it to the influence of Saul of Tarsus, who a little later was to claim the title of church for all the local communities which he had founded? We cannot rule out that possibility. According to Acts, a third peculiarity of the church of Antioch was that it was governed by a college of 'prophets' and 'teachers' who seem to have celebrated a form of worship accompanied by fasting, in the course of which the Holy Spirit manifested itself.[31] In other words, phenomena of supernatural inspiration were very evident in the life of this community, at least within the leading group. Finally, we know from Paul[32] that complete intercommunion was practised between believers of Jewish origin and those of pagan origin, a practice which was accepted without hesitation by Barnabas and even by Peter when he came to Antioch.

In short, some years after its foundation, the church in this city, the result of the missionary enterprise of the Hellenists who had been driven out of Jerusalem, but which had then been taken in hand by emissaries from the mother church, still had quite an original character. It combined features derived from the 'Hellenist' mission with features borrowed from the Jerusalem community and others which resulted from the pressures of the complex setting of a large cosmopolitan city, not to mention the personal influence of Saul of Tarsus. That explains why the missionary campaigns launched from Antioch[33] were no longer based on the 'Hellenist' model but were of a type which we can call

Pauline. We shall return to this later. The verve of Stephen's companions died in this very large city.

However, the example of the Hellenists was very important for setting in motion the evangelization of the world by the disciples of Jesus Christ. Instead of waiting in Jerusalem for the coming of pilgrims from all over the world, and then the return of the Lord, the authorities in the mother church adopted the custom of following in the footsteps of the non-conformist missionaries who went from place to place to preach the gospel. By dint of inspecting and correcting the work of others, they ended up by taking initiatives of their own. The best example of this apprenticeship to missionary mobility is that of Peter: he is an inspector in Samaria on the heels of Philip,[34] then at Lydda and Joppa,[35] and finally at Antioch;[36] we see him become an evangelist in Samaria[37] and then at Caesarea in Palestine,[38] before making himself the unconditional apologist for admitting pagans to the faith.[39] While subsequently he seems to have resumed his role as inspector, for example at Corinth after Paul had been there,[40] there is every reason to think that he was active above all as a missionary,[41] perhaps as far as Anatolia[42] and Rome.[43] Similarly Barnabas, first an inspector in Antioch,[44] subsequently becomes an itinerant evangelist.[45] In short, the 'Hellenists' attracted a following and roused a large number of the leaders in Jerusalem from their initial immobility. Furthermore, we can ask whether the evangelizing passion of the 'Hellenists' did not equally have an effect on Saul of Tarsus. Having set out to extinguish the 'Hellenist' mission in Damascus, after his conversion he was to be found evangelizing Arabia.[46]

So do we have to reduce the 'Hellenists' to activists whose untimely enterprises forced their brothers in the faith to launch out on mission across the world? That would be quite excessive. This anti-establishment group was not content with action. It also reflected on what it was doing and expressed itself in some literary documents in which it defended its choices.

I have already mentioned the commentary on Isaiah 53.7–8 which Philip gives for the Ethiopian eunuch[47] and noted that this is the only passage in the New Testament which interprets this Suffering Servant song as a prediction of the passion of Jesus. Why this somewhat surprising silence, unless the 'Hellenists' had compromised this reading of Second Isaiah by making it a central element in a theology opposed to sacrificial worship?

This is the theology which is expressed in Stephen's speech.[48] This evocation of Israel's past, so original that sometimes a Samaritan tone has been found in it, unexpectedly issues in a regular attack on the Jerusalem Temple. This is followed by a relentless denunciation of the constant opposition on the part of the Jewish leaders to the prophets, to the Righteous One, and to the Law itself. Here we are a very long way from the conciliatory tone employed by Peter in his speeches in Acts 2, 3, 4 and 5. It is no longer a matter of seeking reconciliation with the Temple authorities in order to be tolerated in the sanctuary and to win some of them over to the faith.[49] On the contrary, the objective is to dis-qualify them for ever, to strip them of any authority over the people. The Son of Man standing at the right hand of God who appears to Stephen the moment he finishes his philippic[50] is not simply the future eschatological judge. He is the teacher who is coming from now on to chastize those who persist in their rebellion. We may note once again that this is a portrayal which is unique in the New Testament; the 'Hellenists' prove to be much more violently polemical towards the Jewish rulers than their brothers in the majority church in Jerusalem. Finally, we may note that, contrary to the christocentricity of all the missionary speeches in the Acts of the Apostles, in Stephen's speech we have a christology which is not at all developed: Jesus is called 'the Righteous One'[51] and designated the Son of Man whom God has placed at his right hand after his execution.[52] However, his role as the one who avenges the martyrs does not have the grandeur of that of the Judge at the end of time,[53] which is attributed to him by the christology of the great church. On the contrary, throughout Stephen's speech the notion of God has an extreme majesty, leading up to the emphasis that it is impossible for God to have any other throne than heaven.[54]

These few elements of 'Hellenist' thought remain very scattered and somewhat incoherent. To supplement them and find a more precise expression of this thought we have to look at another document which comes from these circles, the first form of the Gospel of Mark. For a century and a half it has been generally agreed that this Gospel should be recognized as the earliest of the books bearing the name Gospel. On the other hand, the dating of this writing and the existence of a first edition are the object of very lively discussions, of which an account cannot be given here.[55] The absence of any allusion to the Jewish War of 66–70 in the work makes it necessary to date the first edition before 65 and the canonical writing after 75. The author presents his hero as the model for a missionary commitment which will last until the return of the Son of Man, beyond his death and resurrection.[56] He does so in three ways: by stating at the beginning of his book that it is going to be about 'the gospel of Jesus Christ', i.e. the spread of the good news of which Jesus Christ is both the bearer and the subject; by putting the emphasis throughout the work on the missionary activity of Jesus and his disciples rather than on their doctrine; and by concluding his narrative, before the very tightly constructed account of the passion, with an apocalyptic chapter which forms a natural conclusion to it. This is not a christological account or a biographical narrative, but an invitation to follow in the footsteps of Jesus, an itinerant evangelist and healer who was not stopped by any threat. The author of this work uses many traditions about Jesus which he seems to have borrowed from the stock which the mother church used for catechesis, preaching and polemic, but also many miracle stories the fairly crude character of which makes it very improbable that they were used by the church. Since he has left aside many traditions which we find in the passages common to Matthew and Luke, he has therefore composed his book by mixing the church traditions which he wanted to keep with narratives borrowed from popular recollections in Galilee. His evident intention is to present a Jesus who is different from the somewhat stiff teacher whose cult the Jerusalem church had organized. We may also note that he does not hesitate to show the first leaders of this church in a somewhat unpleasant light[57] and to launch virulent attacks on the family of Jesus, including James.[58] This reveals that he is quite hostile to the head of the Jerusalem church. In short, the Gospel of Mark comes from a sphere which knows this church but is not very appreciative of it and does not want to be dependent on it, since it seems to the author to be far too intellectual and ready for all kinds of compromises to achieve the tolerance of the Jewish authorities. The only milieu of this kind that we know is the group of the 'Hellenists'. The Gospel of Mark thus tells us about the thought of this movement. Without going beyond the bounds of probability, we can put its redaction in the region of Caesarea in Palestine, before the end of the 50s CE. The author of the work could have been Philip the evangelist or one of his followers.

Of course there are traces in this Gospel of adaptation to a Roman public to which Palestine was unknown.[59] But these are certainly to be attributed to a new edition of the work aimed at new readers. The passion narrative is totally dominated by the idea that Jesus has to suffer and die alone, whereas chapters 1–13 emphasize the call to suffer and die intrepidly with him. So the passion narrative belongs to this second edition under the name of Mark. Its presence transforms what was an exhortation to bear one's cross after Jesus[60] into a biography offered for readers to meditate on who are complete strangers to the situations which are described for them. The Gospels of Matthew and Luke will take this new logic to its conclusion by relating the life of Jesus from his birth to his death as a biography.

If we keep to the parts of the Gospel of Mark which go back to the first edition, what does this document teach us about the thought of the 'Hellenists'? First of all it confirms that the 'great news' (*euaggelion* in Greek) is both the decisive event of the history of salvation and the message which has to make this event known to all. The preaching of John the Baptist, Jesus and his disciples announces the proximity of the kingdom of God; indeed it is almost confused with this kingdom. As in Paul, the other New Testament author who often speaks of the 'great news', this is mixed up with the action of God in the world;[61] thus it is an eschatological event. It has sometimes been argued that Mark had borrowed this term and this notion from the apostle to the Gentiles. That is not the case. It was Paul who took up the term and the idea as used by the 'Hellenists', since it corresponded to his own convictions about the vital importance of Christian preaching. This indefatigable missionary knew himself to be the instrument of God, as were the 'Hellenists' themselves. For him, as for them, each time the gospel was proclaimed, the merciful judgment of God on the world was given.

Behind this conviction lies a very lofty idea of God. God is not a Creator more or less remote from his creation. He has decided that his kingdom will enter human history and turn it upside down from within. The instrument who brings about this great upheaval is Jesus, by his preaching and his struggle against Satan, but the preachers of the great news also perform this role. Jesus is not a kind of divine being who comes to reveal himself. He is the bearer of the gospel and the combatant who drives back evil and suffering. He is certainly a mysterious being associated with God, but none of the titles used by the disciples of the first generation to describe his person and his function is truly adequate. The evangelist mentions them in passing, but does not put the emphasis on any of them. Neither 'Christ' (seven occurrences) nor 'Son of God' (between five and seven occurrences) is very important. 'Teacher' (twelve occurrences, to which we can add three occurrences of *rabbi* and one of *rabbouni*) and 'Son of Man' are more so, but they do not have a very clear christological meaning. Basically, what identifies the figure of Jesus best is the attitude of those who encounter him, which is one of amazed wonder,[62] unconditional obedience[63] and absolute trust. These features underline the exceptional importance of the liberating mission entrusted by God to Jesus rather than Jesus' nature and identity. So one cannot say that the christological thought in the Gospel of Mark is very developed, as it is, for example, in the Fourth Gospel. What is at the centre in Mark is the drastic intervention of God in the world, of which Jesus is the principal agent. The disciples will join with him and then succeed him. The suffering and the death of Jesus which the threefold prediction of Mark (8.31–32; 9.31; 10.32–34) emphasizes most insistently is part of the mission received from God and shares in the very nature of the kingdom which it inaugurates. This has nothing to do with the power of human rulers.[64] A kingdom of service, it is also a kingdom of freedom, through the emancipation which the Son of Man secures for the many through the gift of his life.[65] Thus liberated, men and women can from now on accept the gospel without Satan being able to oppose it. The call to the disciples to lose their lives in turn for their Teacher and the gospel[66] is all the more pressing.

There is no indication that the free life thus offered to the subjects of the kingdom of God would be a life without law. Contrary to what has sometimes been argued, the Gospel of Mark is not addressed to readers invited to live in disregard of the Law of Moses. Certainly the rules of ritual purity are vigorously criticized in the Gospel, as is also the authority of the oral tradition;[67] the practice of fasting is also put in question,[68] as is that of the *shabbat*[69] and of divorce;[70] the Temple is denounced as an institution which has become sterile.[71] However, it is not the Law that is being attacked, but the customs which have been grafted on to it. These Jesus criticizes as human traditions which distort the profound meaning of the Mosaic commandments. In short, it is the oral law in process of formation that is the object of the attacks of Jesus relayed by the evangelist. By contrast the written Law is mentioned with the utmost respect[72] and remains the indubitable moral point of reference. Since with very rare exceptions[73] those who meet Jesus are Jews, it is clear that this Gospel, too, is addressed to Jews for whom the Law remains fully valid in its written form as interpreted by the Master.

However, since the kingdom has come so near that it turns the order of the world upside down,[74] for some this obedience to the law becomes a pressing call to heroism and self-sacrifice in order to continue the spread of the gospel.[75] Contrary to the attitude of the Jerusalem church, passive in the expectation of an imminent parousia, the circles whom Mark addresses engage in unlimited activity to ensure the presence of the kingdom of God from now on. The eschatological fulfilment that the coming of the Son of Man will bring[76] will merely make this kingdom stable and visible. It will not arrive as soon as the people in Jerusalem think. So it is important to wait for it without any particular fever, as is shown by the interminable list of preludes which form the substance of chapter 13.

In short, the Gospel of Mark introduces us to the thought of the 'Hellenists' in a much more precise way than the other texts which mention them. It confirms that this group was activist, rather than inclined to theological reflection. That doubtless explains why it did not survive the passing of the years. Once the first generation had disappeared, the extraordinary dynamism of the first missionaries rapidly declined. Those of the 'Hellenist' communities of Palestine and Syria which survived fell into a lethargy which led to their progressive disappearance under the thrust of rival groups which were better equipped to last. After Paul's visits to Tyre, Ptolemais and Caesarea[77] around 58 we have no further trace of the existence of communities of this tendency. This vigorously anti-establishment movement thus had quite a short history. However, it bequeathed some important features to subsequent Christian generations. It forced the Jerusalem church to emerge from its cocoon and take an interest in the world outside, in order to avoid the troublesome deviations which had been the starting point for the mission organized around Peter. It contributed to the Hellenization of Christianity on a cultural level, and this directed its expansion towards the Roman empire rather than to the Semitic East. Moreover, the first edition of the Gospel of Mark offered a literary model which had such an attraction for the Christian authors of the second and third generations that the Gospel became the favourite mode of expression of Christian faith. These are by no means small achievements for people whose culture was far less developed than their missionary zeal.

5

Paul, The First Steps

Paul is both the best-known figure of the first Christian generation and a man who in many respects remains mysterious. At least seven of his letters are indisputably authentic, while several others at any rate contain information about the author cited in the superscription. These are an exceptional source of knowledge of the person who wrote them. After introducing Paul in chapters 8, 9 and 11, the Acts of the Apostles devotes almost the whole of the second part, from chapter 13 on, to him. However, the authentic letters are distributed over only fifteen years at most, and the account in Acts, written some twenty years after the death of Paul, has such an apologetic colouring that we need to be rigorously critical if we are to get reliable evidence out of it. In short, our documentary wealth remains quite relative, and many questions about Paul will remain unanswered or will find only hypothetical solutions.[1]

The date of Paul's birth is unknown, but it was doubtless shortly before 10 CE. He came from a Jewish family living in Tarsus in Cilicia, a very lively city in which there was great intellectual activity. At birth, according to the custom current in the Jewish families of the Diaspora, he was given the biblical name Saul and the very Roman name of Paul. His father, who seems to have acquired Roman citizenship in circumstances unknown to us,[2] wanted in this way to show his attachment to a member of the gens of the Pauli, who had rendered him a service in one way or another. Paul's Roman citizenship has sometimes been put in question, since he does not make the slightest allusion to it in his letters. However, the reasons invoked to support such radical scepticism about the statements in the Acts of the Apostles[3] are unconvincing. Furthermore we shall see that Paul, complete Jew that he was, had a very marked liking for everything Roman, and this is doubtless connected with his membership of the group of citizens of the City, which was still not very large in the East.

We do not know anything about Paul's physical appearance. The only features of a portrait that we have come from the end of the second century[4] and are merely the expression of the ascetic leanings of the author of this legendary work. On the other hand, Paul does not seem to have enjoyed very good health: he had evangelized the Galatians when he was very sick[5] and seems to have suffered from a chronic and painful disease.[6] We do not know what it was, but it was an obstacle to his activity. Around 58–60 he was already describing himself as an old man.[7] It is true that he had not been looking after himself for twenty-five years,[8] so by the age of fifty he could have felt prematurely aged.

Like his family, this Diaspora Jew had observed the Jewish law very faithfully. He calls himself a Pharisee,[9] 'circumcised the eight day',[10] 'as to the justice to be found in the law, beyond reproach'.[11] According to the Acts of the Apostles he is even a 'Pharisee, son of Pharisees'.[12] His letters attest that he had received a Greek education but also that in his youth he had benefited from the teaching of the rabbis. The Acts of the Apostles add the detail that he had been the pupil of Rabbi Gamaliel the Elder in Jerusalem,[13] and there is nothing impossible about this. It is also probable that he knew Aramaic,[14] even if Greek was his mother tongue. Doubtless he spent a good deal of his youth in Jerusalem and took part in the discussions provoked by the execution of Jesus and the settlement of Jesus' disciples in the capital.

Again, when the 'Hellenists' seized their autonomy from the majority church and launched on a campaign of evangelization among the Greek-speaking Jews who had settled in Jerusalem, Paul was among the activists who lynched Stephen[15] and then energetically sought to suppress Stephen's supporters.[16] He never tries to disguise his activity as a persecutor.[17] He even speaks in this connection of the 'zeal' which inspired him.[18] We can ask whether this zeal to defend 'the traditions of the fathers' did not make him a Zealot in the strictest sense of this term,[19] i.e. a member of the party with this name which resorted to violent action in defence of God's honour. Two strange episodes mentioned in Acts might be support for this hypothesis. In Acts 9.26–30 Paul has great difficulty in meeting up with the Jerusalem church and finally has to flee in order to escape death threats; in Acts 23.12–22, more than forty Jews take a vow to kill Paul, then a prisoner of the Romans. In both cases we have the feeling that Paul has to die because he has betrayed a solemn commitment to a secret society; this fits what we know about the organization of the Zealot party very well. Furthermore, the moment that he sets out on his last visit to Jerusalem, Paul himself expresses the hope of escaping the unbelievers in Judaea,[20] which suggests that he feared for his life on his journey there. So it is reasonable to assume that the young Paul belonged to a secret society related to the Zealot movement and that in the eyes of his old accomplices his desertion after the event on the Damascus road was punishable by death.

This is the framework within which we have to understand the mission entrusted to the young Zealot sent to Damascus to do away there with possible disciples of the 'Hellenist' agitators who challenged the Temple and announced its destruction.[21] There is no substance to the objections made to the historicity of this episode if we recall that here we have an example of Zealot initiative which may perhaps have been backed by the high priest, but was by no means strictly legal. However, we must be careful not to do more than recognize the general probability of the mission entrusted to Paul. The details in 9.2 derive from the redaction of Acts.

The dramatic episode which took place on the approach to Damascus[22] is never related by Paul in his letters. Only in Galatians (1.15–16) does the apostle mention the revelation by God of his Son in him, and this seems to refer more to an inner upheaval than to a spectacular manifestation like that related in the Acts of the Apostles.[23] Furthermore, Paul is content to liken the appearance of the Risen Christ which he received to those granted previously to the accredited witnesses to the resurrection.[24] He mentions an external event, but without embarking on any narrative. In short, the narrative in Acts has often been regarded as the legendary embellishment, markedly inspired by the literary genre of the divine appearance in Hellenistic literature, of a fact about which Paul had remained very reticent. Beyond question the author of Acts has embroidered the theme of the appearance of the Risen Christ to Paul somewhat, since he gives three accounts of it. These contain important variants[25] intended, at least in part, to integrate them into the three contexts where he has put them. However, the redactional intervention of the author is not sufficient to explain all the differences that can be noted between these three accounts of the same event.

The key to the problem thus posed lies in the account of the intervention of Ananias. This is absent from chapter 26, but is related in Acts 9.10–19 and 22.12–16. If we remove various redactional elements, we can see that this is a healing story of the most common kind. It describes the duration and gravity of the illness (9.9); the waiting of the sick person (9.12); the approach of the healer (9.17; 22.13); a gesture which brings about the healing and a saying which goes with it (ibid.); the suddenness of the healing (9.18–22.13); proof of the reality of the healing (9.18); and a new start for the sick person who has been healed (9.18–19; 22.13). There is every reason to think that this is a traditional account of a healing which the author of Acts has collected. The presentation of the sick person which should have begun this story surely alluded to the reasons for Paul's blindness, making a brief mention of the appearance of the Risen Christ. The developed form that the appearance has taken in Acts 9.3–8 and 22.6–11 is the product of the redactional activity of the author of Acts, who has made use of the narrative in 26.13–15 to reinforce this element which seemed particularly important to him. So in chapters 9 and 22 there is a combination of two traditions of very different provenance: an account of the healing of Paul by Ananias, formed in the Damascus church; and a narration of the appearance of the Risen Christ to Paul, which in all probability comes from the circle of Paul's disciples and could well be based on confidences entrusted by the apostle to those around him.[26]

So what happened on the Damascus road? Paul was floored and blinded by a dazzling light at high noon, heard the voice of a supernatural being asking why Paul was persecuting him, and then learned that this was Jesus, who finally gave him instructions. In chapter 26, these instructions relate to his mission to the Jews and the pagans to win them over to the faith (26.16–18), whereas in chapters 9 and 22 they are simply that he should go to Damascus, there to learn what to do (9.6; 22.10). It is Ananias who restores his sight, baptizes him and tells him that he is to be a witness of God to men and women (22.14–15; this remains implicit in chapter 9). Psychologists, historians and theologians have commented on this 'conversion' of Paul, the suddenness of which certainly reveals that he was in the grips of a violent inner debate. At all events, one mistake in interpretation which should not be made is to see this sudden shift as a change of religion. Even if from then on Paul understood his mission as being the evangelization of pagans alone, as he suggests in Galatians (1.16), everything indicates that he continued to preach to the Jews whenever possible. Furthermore Paul feels more Jewish than ever after his baptism: it was the God of Israel who sent him to preach the gospel. Indeed, he felt this so strongly that one day he would come to present himself as the new Elijah charged with raising up the remnant of Israel to ensure the continuity of the chosen people, despite its revolt,[27] and allow the return of the rebels to God.[28] Thus, far from signifying a change of religion, Paul's conversion signifies his sudden discovery of his true place in the life of Israel.

We do not know the date of this important event. On the basis of the indications given by Paul in Galatians (1.18 and 2.1) we can venture the hypothesis that it was in 33–35 CE, i.e. a few years after the formation of the first church in Jerusalem. Thus Paul is very much part of the first generation of Christians, and even if he did not know Jesus personally (II Corinthians 5.16 does not allow us to affirm this), he is a contemporary of the first disciples both by birth and by his becoming a believer.

Hardly had Paul been converted than he threw himself headlong into evangelization. After a brief spell in Damascus, he went to Arabia, i.e. present-day Jordan,[29] there to preach the gospel in conditions about which we know nothing. On his return to Damascus somewhat later, he also preached there, according to Acts (9.20–22) in the synagogues. He seems to have had such a striking message that in both these places violent oppositions arose, so much so that he had to flee secretly from Damascus in bizarre circumstances in order to escape the police of King Aretas of Arabia[30] and perhaps the vengeance of Jewish plotters[31] whose behaviour resembled that of the Zealots. Fifteen to twenty years later Paul was not very proud of this episode,[32] which had brought him severe criticism from the Christians of Damascus. We have no information about the content of the gospel which Paul had sought to spread during this period. The ambiguous formula of Galatians 5.11, which could conjure up Paul's Jewish past, could also refer to his beginnings as a Christian preacher. The apostle would then have begun his missionary activity without exempting the pagans he had won over to faith in Christ from the circumcision which later he did so much to spare them. One hesitates to attribute such an attitude to Paul, even at the beginning. However, it remains a possibility.

Three years after the event on the Damascus road, the young preacher, quite shaken by the unfavourable circumstances, decided to go to Jerusalem, where he found further resources to help him resume his course. He went there to get to know Peter, with whom he stayed two weeks.[33] Doubtless Peter taught him certain features of the oral tradition about Jesus,[34] of the christological interpretation of the prophets and of the confessions of faith. This visit remained quite confidential, since the only other leader of the church whom Paul got to see was 'James, the brother of the Lord'.[35] The Acts of the Apostles explains the small number of meetings which Paul had by the mistrust which still existed towards him, since he had been known only as a persecutor of the church.[36] It has Barnabas, an esteemed member of the community, intervening on his behalf.[37] Thanks to this support, Paul will have shared the life of the apostles for a while until the time when, again threatened with assassination, he took flight in the direction of Caesarea and then Tarsus, his home town.[38] In short, Paul had been enriched by contact with the mother church, but had not succeeded in becoming integrated into it by reason of his Zealot past.

We know nothing of Paul's activities in Tarsus. Doubtless he resumed his craft of 'tentmaker',[39] while proclaiming his faith in the synagogue whenever possible. However, we do not know what results he was able to achieve. One might suppose that he propagated the sound Jerusalem doctrine into which he had just been initiated. This stay in Tarsus could have lasted for several years. Certainly it was also a period of personal maturing for Paul, who had hardly paused since his conversion.

When, towards the beginning of the 40s, Barnabas was sent to Antioch by the Jerusalem church to take in hand the community founded there by the 'Hellenist' missionaries, he found so much to do that he went to find Paul in Tarsus, some 150 miles north-west of the great Syrian city. Paul followed him to Antioch, and with him became one of the leaders of the local church.[40] For a year the two men worked together spreading the gospel in Antioch, apparently with much success.[41] Did they then go to Jerusalem to bring aid intended to help their brethren in the capital who had been struck by famine? This is what Acts says,[42] linking this mission to a great famine which hit the Roman empire in the reign of Claudius, who was emperor from 41 to 54 CE. It came to a climax between 46 and 48.[43] However, the two passages in Acts which mention this journey are very allusive and Paul says nothing of such a move in his letters. So there are serious doubts, even if this episode remains possible, above all if one accepts that it is being confused with Acts 15.2ff.

The departure of Barnabas and Paul as envoys of the church of Antioch designated by the Holy Spirit is much better attested and was much more decisive.[44] This form of designation is not given any particular explanation. All we know is that the Holy Spirit speaks during an assembly for worship, accompanied by fasting, of the five 'prophets and teachers' who are exercising their ministry in the church of Antioch. Doubtless this supernatural declaration was made by one of the local prophets. The divine voice commands that Barnabas and Paul should be chosen for God with a view to the work to which he has called them. So they must leave the service of the community to perform another task; this is known to them but not specified in other ways. This statement looks very much like the conclusion to a discussion between the two parties concerned, who have heard a call, and their companions in charge of the local church, who find it difficult to lose two essential colleagues. Once the decision has been taken there is more fasting, prayer, the laying on of hands on the two who are leaving, and a farewell. All this supports the impression of a firmly organized community which does not allow itself to be troubled by the sense of vocation in any of its leaders, but pays attention when collective inspiration comes to confirm this personal feeling.

Thus released from their obligations towards the church of Antioch, Barnabas and Paul take the sea route, embark at Seleucia and set sail for Cyprus. It is again the Holy Spirit which sends them in this direction,[45] but we are not told how this order had been received. We can imagine that Barnabas, who came from Cyprus,[46] had kept up some connections there and thought that it would be favourable ground for their preaching. At Salamis, a port facing the Syrian coast which had formerly been the capital of the island of Cyprus, the two preachers proclaim the gospel in the synagogue, but we are not told what success they had.[47] At this point we learn that they had with them an assistant, John. Just beforehand we had been told[48] that he had recently come from Jerusalem and bore the surname Mark.[49] Doubtless this is meant to indicate to us that Salamis was a place where the harvest looked like being excellent.

After a stay of uncertain duration in Salamis, Barnabas, Paul and John cross the island from east to west. We do not know whether they preached *en route*. They arrive at Paphos, the great port on the west coast of the island and the residence of the Roman governor.[50] The account which Acts gives of their stay in this city is strange.[51] No public preaching is mentioned, whether in a synagogue or elsewhere. The encounter with a Jewish magician, also described as a false prophet and bearing two different names (Bar Jesus in v.6 and Elymas in v.8), is not explained, and the incident which sets Paul against this bizarre figure has a totally legendary appearance. We may simply note that Paul, hitherto subordinate to Barnabas, here takes the main role. The proconsul Sergius Paulus, an 'intelligent man' who becomes a believer after meeting the two missionaries at his own request, is also a figure coloured with legend, though there could have been a proconsul of this name on Cyprus. The author of Acts takes advantage of this encounter to slip in the name Paul, which from now on he uses instead of Saul to designate his hero. That allows him to emphasize the apostle's love of Rome, and the favourable attitude of a Roman of high rank towards the Christian faith. Furthermore, Paul's firmness towards a magician here corresponds to that of Peter towards Simon.[52] This is a good illustration of the parallelism which the author of Acts seeks to establish between the two apostles. In short, the skilful use of a legend and the intense redactional activity of the author have swallowed up the few facts here. These doubtless referred to the establishment of a Christian community in Paphos.

On leaving this city by sea, Barnabas and Paul went north-west to Perga in Pamphylia. They do not seem to have stopped there, although it was a large Greek-speaking city.[53] The only incident related in this place is the desertion of John Mark, who returned from there to Jerusalem, apparently to Paul's great displeasure.[54] The reasons for this premature departure are not given. We may ask whether the paradoxical decision of the two missionaries not to engage in mission in Pamphylia but rather to leave immediately for the high plain of Anatolia, a kind of barbarian frontier, contributed to this break.

In fact, it is quite difficult to explain this choice. For evangelists who came from Cyprus and Cilicia or Antioch in Syria, Pamphylia, a rich coastal plain steeped in Greek culture, with its great commercial cities, should have been a tempting mission field. There must have been a strong reason for neglecting it, but the texts tell us nothing about this. It has sometimes been thought that the health of the two men could have been a reason: they might have suffered from malaria, so that to stay in this partly marshy plain could have been harmful.[55] However, crossing the Taurus chain to reach the plain of Anatolia involved a journey which was long and dangerous because of the steep contours and the frequent presence of brigands. Such an expedition would not have been tempting for sick men. So we cannot avoid noting that Barnabas and Paul took a surprising decision. The only possible explanation is that the two missionaries aimed at places whose links with Rome were particularly strong. Pisidian Antioch, their first destination beyond the Taurus, had just been given the status of a Roman colony under Italian law. The city was situated on the Via Sebaste, which linked Ephesus with the high valley of the Euphrates and from it roads ran giving access through the Taurus chain to Cilicia and northern Syria. Lystra was also a Roman colony; Derbe had just obtained a special status from the emperor Claudius similar to that of the colonies.

Finally, Iconium was scheming actively with Rome to obtain the same privileges as Derbe; it eventually received these at the end of the reign of Claudius. It commanded the route crossing the Taurus in the direction of the port of Seleucia and its junction with the Via Sebaste. In short, these were strategic bases which allowed Rome to control the land routes between West and East. By all accounts, it was Paul who led Barnabas into these regions which were semi-desert, but which formed the hinterland of Tarsus. Did he do this with the support of the pro-consul of Cyprus,[56] who perhaps had links with this southern part of the province of Galatia, which combined with Galatia proper the districts of Lycaonia, Pisidia and Pamphylia? It would be rash to claim this, but the question is worth asking, given the lack of any really satisfactory explanation of the direction taken by the two missionaries.

The events of this missionary journey in southern Galatia as reported in Acts 13.14 to 14.27 are not worth relating in full. However, a number of points are significant enough to pause over. In the first two cities in which the two missionaries stopped, Pisidian Antioch and Iconium, there were relatively large Jewish communities, and Barnabas and Paul began their preaching in the synagogues. They had real success, among both the Jews and the proselytes and sympathizers who took part in synagogue worship. However, the Jews for the most part rapidly regained control and launched a violent campaign against Barnabas and Paul. With the support of the municipal authorities they succeeded in banishing the missionaries from their territory. In the next two cities, Lystra and Derbe, where there was no synagogue, the preaching was addressed to all the population. However, it was interrupted at Lystra by the intervention of Jews coming from Pisidian Antioch and Iconium. When they got to Derbe, the two evangelists retraced their steps; we are not told why. Their aim could have been the organization of stable communities in the four cities which they had evangelized; in each of these churches were 'elders' designated by the missionaries, in conformity to the Jerusalem model.[57] It should also be noted that the title 'apostles' is twice[58] given to Barnabas and Paul, whereas the definition of the apostolate given in Acts 1.21–22 would seem to exclude them from the number of the apostles. There is an inconsistency here on the part of the author of Acts which suggests that the definition of apostle had become narrower around 80–85 CE than in the time of the first generation. Doubtless, for several decades, being sent on mission by the Holy Spirit and the leaders of a community was enough to make a missionary an apostle, but then the embarrassment caused in communities by itinerant apostles who did not have authentic authority necessitated a more restrictive definition. We shall return later to the importance attached by Paul to the recognition of his dignity as an apostle. The author of Acts, who wanted to limit the apostolic circle as far as possible to the group of the Twelve, did not dare to deprive him of this title entirely, but gives it to him only in these two passages of chapter 14.

Once they had accomplished their task of setting up the four communities in southern Galatia, the two apostles resumed the coastal route. They preached the word at Perga, though we are not told of the creation of a community in this city, and then embarked at Attalia to return to Antioch. There they reported to the brethren, above all about how pagans had accepted the faith, and resumed their place in the life of the church.[59] How long they had been away is difficult to say: at all events several months and probably more than a year. Doubtless another similar missionary journey was envisaged for later.[60]

However, a series of events was to interrupt this rhythm and lead to the break-up of the team formed by Barnabas and Paul. The accounts of these episodes given in Acts[61] and the letter to the Galatians[62] differ significantly, and force the historian to make difficult critical choices. It all began with the arrival at Antioch of Christians from Judaea. They asserted that circumcision was necessary for salvation and sought to spread their ideas within the community. Paul and Barnabas opposed them, doubtless strengthened by the positive results of their journey of evangelization. Without dismissing their thesis, the community decided that it was necessary to obtain the opinion of the apostles and the elders in Jerusalem and formed a delegation which left for the Jewish capital. Paul and Barnabas were members of it, but other believers accompanied them;[63] this doubtless shows some reservations about the views of the two missionaries. Paul, who does not mention other members of the Antiochene delegation, adds a chronological detail which is unfortunately difficult to interpret. This journey took place 'fourteen years afterwards';[64] however, we do not know whether these fourteen years are reckoned from Paul's previous journey to Jerusalem[65] or from his conversion, three years before this first journey.[66] Since this second hypothesis is rather more probable, we may take 48 CE as an acceptable approximation.[67]

The account of the meeting in Jerusalem that we read in Acts 15 doubtless contains some authentic details, but it bears the stamp of Lukan redaction. It is better to trust the narrative in Galatians 2.1–10, even if Paul presents the facts in an apologetic way. The initial test is the acceptance by the Christian leaders in Jerusalem of the Greek Titus as a brother on whom no conditions had to be imposed. He accompanied Paul and Barnabas and had not been circumcised. Paul is all the more relieved since an offensive had been launched to have Titus circumcised by those whom he calls 'false brethren who crept in', seeking to remove the Christian freedom that was practised around Paul and Barnabas.[68] These 'false brethren' were doubtless the 'people from Judaea' who according to Acts 15.1 had disturbed the peace of the church. Once their attacks have been disposed of, Paul turns to the leaders of the church and notes that they at least sought a reasonable compromise. First they acknowledged that both Peter and Paul had received a missionary vocation: Peter to the circumcised and Paul to the uncircumcised. Here Paul alludes to the event on the Damascus road in his own case, but with Peter things are less clear; perhaps the reference is to his function as spokesman of the group of disciples on the day of Pentecost. Clearly it is not to his vision in Joppa,[69] which according to Acts makes Peter the initiator of the mission to the pagans.[70] Be this as it may, it is the missionary Peter to whom Paul refers here, some years after his clandestine departure from Jerusalem in 44. The parallelism between Peter and Paul serves as the basis for an agreement between the 'pillars' in Jerusalem, James, Cephas and John, on the one hand, and Paul and Barnabas on the other. The mission field is shared, with the evangelization of the Jews being entrusted to the former and that of the pagans to the latter.[71] This very simple formula perhaps has various connotations, like for example the idea that communities bringing together Jews and pagans who have been won over to Christ are not desirable. We shall be returning to that. It should also be noted that James, who is cited as head of the 'pillars', is accompanied by Cephas (who must be identified with the Peter of vv. 7 and 8 since the first of these two names is the transcription and the second the translation of the surname *Kepha* given by Jesus to his disciple Simon), and John, who must certainly be identified with the son of Zebedee. John had formed a circle around him which was somewhat on the periphery of the majority church. The head of the church, the missionary authority and the theologian unite in granting Paul and Barnabas a recognition which is perhaps somewhat condescending, in return for the sending of aid to the 'poor', i.e. the Christians of Jerusalem who have no resources.

The compromise suggested by James, and according to Acts ratified by the Jerusalem church (15.19–29), is incompatible with the account in

Galatians (2.1–10). As it was widely implemented in the second century, its authenticity can hardly be doubted, but its origin could well lie later than the meeting in 48. The incident at Antioch which Paul relates in Galatians 2.11–13 reveals that in James' eyes the recognition of the ministry of Paul and Barnabas in no way implied a common life which brought together believers of Jewish origin and converts of pagan origin. Peter and Barnabas, whose personal interpretation was more flexible, then aligned themselves with James' position. Paul discovered to his great indignation that the Jerusalem agreement made communion between the two categories of Christians impossible in these conditions. We shall be returning to the radical conclusions which he drew from this. But beyond doubt his fury made James and those around him think. They then tried to save the mixed churches by demanding that converts of pagan origin should submit to certain rules inspired by the Noachic commandments which Judaism presented to sympathizers who wanted to come to the synagogues. They were to avoid associations with idolatrous cults or eating pagan sacrificial meat; they were not to engage in unions which according to the law of Moses were illicit; and they were not to consume meat with blood in it or blood itself. Thus communion with them would no longer condemn Christian Jews to defile themselves, and mixed churches would again become possible. These rules, proposed some time after the incident at Antioch to the churches of Syria and Cilicia, doubtless reflected their desire to retain the mixed communities which had been established in these provinces. The extension of them later to all the churches marked the victory of a conciliatory Jewish Christianity which we may put between 70 and 90 CE.

Neither Paul nor his heirs accepted this compromise, which had been decided without their participation. For them, Christian freedom was a principle over which no prevarication was possible. Thus for Paul, fifteen years after he became a Christian, a new period of his career began.

6

Paul, Flight Forward

The incident at Antioch had shown Paul the Jerusalemite interpretation of the agreement approved earlier in the Jewish capital.[1] Certainly, Paul and Barnabas had been recognized as legitimate missionaries to the pagans; certainly, no special demands like circumcision were to be imposed on the pagan converts; however, it did not follow from that that Jewish Christians and their brethren of pagan origin could live in full communion. Each of these two groups had to form its own community. This restrictive point of view was so solidly based that Peter and Barnabas himself, Paul's faithful companion, recognized its validity and broke communion with the brethren of pagan origin who lived in Antioch.[2] That was a disaster for Paul. The highest Christian authorities regarded the salvation brought by Jesus Christ as secondary to the ethnic status of the converts. In his eyes this was a scandal, indeed an unacceptable swindle inflicted on him and on all Christians of pagan origin. No compromise was possible with James and all those who had supported his position.

So there was a break. It was a break with James and the Jerusalem church. It was a break with Peter, whose vacillation over an essential question was denounced with vigour.[3] It was a break with Barnabas, Paul's old companion, though he continued the missionary enterprise.[4] And it was a break with the church of Antioch itself, within which almost no one seems to have taken Paul's side. Paul did not return there for many years according to Acts;[5] perhaps never, if one doubts the substance of this very brief note. Only Silas, though a Jerusalemite, joined Paul for new missionary adventures,[6] while some Antiochene brethren doubtless still continued to have trust in him.

There was perhaps another reason for the extreme brutality of the break brought about by Paul, who thus deprived himself of any base for his missionary enterprises. If, as is probable, the Letter to the Galatians is addressed to the Christians of south Galatia, those of Pisidian Antioch, Iconium, Lystra and Derbe who had been evangelized two or three years earlier by Barnabas and Paul, everything suggests that it was written at the time of the incident at Antioch or shortly afterwards, when Paul's indignation was at its height.⁷ It then shows us that James' emissaries had not only been sent to restore order in Antioch but had also set about normalizing the situation existing in these very young churches, whose founders had encouraged them to practise full communion between circumcised and uncircumcised. This was all the more logical since these were small communities which it would have been absurd to split. With the same logic as Paul and Barnabas, the intruders seem to have argued that the small size of the communities made it necessary for them to maintain their unity, and this was possible only if the non-Jews submitted to the Law. This admonition to observe the Law naturally led to the acceptance of circumcision, which alone could make converted pagan males brothers of believers who came from Judaism, and which moreover allowed the community to remain under the wing of the synagogue and its privileged status.

In the Letter to the Galatians, Paul counters these opportunist arguments with fundamental objections. According to him, the former pagans who agreed to submit to the Mosaic Law in order to facilitate community life were showing how little importance they attached to the divine promise made to all believers, to the gift of the Holy Spirit and the freedom which results from it. They were making themselves guilty of a real denial which would invalidate the gift that God gave them in Jesus Christ. They were going over to 'another gospel',⁸ which had no reality and which 'reverses the gospel of Christ'.⁹ As for anyone who propagates such teaching, incompatible with that of Paul, 'let him be anathema'!¹⁰ The fact that these intruders appealed to the Jerusalem church should not impress anyone. The gospel proclaimed by Paul was of divine origin and moreover was recognized as such by the leaders of the Jerusalem church.¹¹ The theological developments that Paul presents in support of this intransigent thesis are well known: new life in faith in Christ;¹² the gift of the Spirit to those who have this faith;¹³ the priority of the divine promise over the Law;¹⁴ the access of believers to freedom since the coming of Christ;¹⁵ the covenant of freedom as opposed to the covenant of slavery;¹⁶ the Christian life as a free expression of the Spirit given to believers.¹⁷ Expounded here in a somewhat disorderly and very abrupt way, these themes would be taken up in other letters of Paul, refined and developed in masterly fashion. See especially the Letter to the Romans, written some ten years later and with more leisure, where all these ideas recur in an impressive synthesis.

Paul writes passionately to these few Galatian communities born out

of his missionary activity, taking up the pen himself.[18] He expresses
the wish that he could come to them, so that he could persuade his
correspondents better to listen to him.[19] And in fact some time later it
was for the cities of southern Galatia that he left Antioch.[20] Acts relates
that Silas, his companion, and he made known the conclusions of the
Jerusalem meeting in all the cities through which they passed.[21] We
are obliged to qualify this statement: this was not the compromise
suggested by James,[22] which was certainly later, but rather the mutual
recognition of the ministries of Peter and Paul.[23] Another episode in this
narrative in Acts, that of the circumcision of Timothy,[24] surprises the
reader of Galatians. Do we have to deny its historicity? Perhaps not. Son
of a Jewish mother, in the eyes of the members of the synagogues
Timothy was a Jew. If he remained uncircumcised at the moment of
undertaking the career of an itinerant missionary, he risked being
denounced as an apostate and having trouble with the Jewish tribunals
which functioned in the synagogues. By refusing to circumcise Titus,[25]
who was of pagan origin, Paul had defended Christian freedom. By
circumcising a Jew who was going to enter numerous synagogues to
preach the gospel there, he was adopting a pragmatic attitude, which he
was capable of doing whenever no matter of principle was involved.

Whatever we may make of this episode, Paul does not seem to have
had too much difficulty in putting the churches of southern Galatia on
the right road.[26] He had thus found a new base, though it was modest
by comparison with the great church of Antioch in Syria. But he knew
that he was called to go much further, and after some time he resumed
his journey. The Acts of the Apostles[27] is the only source to inform us,
albeit summarily, about the first part of this new journey, as far as the
city of Philippi in Macedonia. Thus this short passage deserves attentive
and critical reading. We should first note that between southern Galatia
and Troas, a port and Roman colony situated on the north-west coast
of Anatolia, Paul and his companions covered several hundred miles on
foot, over the sparsely populated and remote plains of Phrygia. This was
certainly the most economical way to travel. Doubtless the missionaries'
purse was quite thin without the support of a great church, and that
prompted them to avoid the costs of a journey by sea. They only
resolved on such a voyage after the call for help from a Macedonian
which Paul heard in Troas. However, there are more surprises in this
account. During this long journey by land, there is no mention of any
preaching of the gospel, as though the missionaries were *en route* for a
propitious place in which to preach. Now this place was neither Asia

nor Bithynia, with their great Greek-speaking cities, as they learned on the way from revelations of the Holy Spirit, though these were attractive objectives. It was not even Troas, where Paul preached only several years later.[28] It was to be Macedonia, as was suggested by the vision which Paul saw in Troas and as the group of missionaries was convinced when they heard about this dream. By all accounts the author of Acts is intrigued by this strange quest for a suitable missionary objective and can only explain it by a divine plan revealed to Paul bit by bit. Without putting in question Paul's constant submission to directives from on high, we may ask whether from his departure from southern Galatia the apostle did not have just one idea in his head, using the successive inspirations which came to him *en route* to lead his colleagues, who were keen to go into action, further and further. Aware of the weakness of his new base and the magnitude of the task with which God was entrusting him among the pagans, he wanted to go to Rome to make this city the centre of the evangelization of the non-Jews, as a counter-balance to Jerusalem, the centre of the mission to the Jews. This grandiose project was to be thwarted by the circumstances, but the Letter to the Romans, written a mere ten years later, attests that it was never completely dropped by Paul.[29] So Macedonia was only a stage, albeit a stage which, situated as it was half-way between southern Galatia and Rome, brought him much nearer to his goal. By the Via Egnatia, which crossed this province from east to west as far as the Adriatic, access to Italy was easy; it involved only a short and therefore cheap sea crossing. Moreover Macedonian churches could take over from the small communities of southern Galatia and provide the group around Paul with the necessary resources for continuing his progress.

As in southern Galatia and Troas, after their disembarkation in Macedonia Paul and his companions did not turn to the more important cities, but to a Roman colony, Philippi. This small city, populated by Roman veterans and Latin peasants, with very few Jews and no synagogue, was their first mission field since their departure from southern Galatia around 50 CE. A strange way of responding to the call of the Macedonian whom Paul saw in a dream at Troas! But this choice was logical if they were looking for a stopping point on the route to Rome. A Jewish place of prayer outside the city was the starting point for the evangelization of Philippi. The women gathered there received the preaching favourably. In particular a certain Lydia, a purple merchant who came from Thyatira, a city in the province of Asia known as a great centre for dyeing, had herself baptized by the missionaries and gave them lodgings during their stay in Philippi. A Christian community formed rapidly. It was to become one of those most faithful to Paul, for whom it showed remarkably constant affection and for whom it provided material aid.[30] Paul seems to have been anxious to celebrate the Passover there some years later, before finally leaving the region of the Aegean Sea.[31] It will also be noted that the account of Paul's first stay in Philippi is the first passage in Acts to be written in the first person plural, the 'we' appearing in the discussion of the meaning of his vision at Troas.[32] This redaction in the first person plural could be a literary artifice, but it is more probable that it comes from a source which has been reproduced literally. Since this source has all the appearance of being a travel diary of the group of missionaries around Paul, aimed at recording the main everyday events, we may suppose that the account here is very close to the facts.[33]

One incident came to disturb the peaceful progress of the gospel in Philippi. A young servant girl endowed with powers of divination began to follow Paul and his companions, ceaselessly crying out that these men were bringing salvation. In the end, Paul, exhausted by all the fuss, exorcised the girl.[34] This provoked the wrath of her masters, who had thus been deprived of a substantial source of revenue. Dragged before the magistrates, Paul and Silas were beaten and thrown in prison. However, an earthquake liberated them the following night, and the shock of it led to the gaoler's conversion.[35] When day came they were freed, but were asked to leave the city. This they did after resuming contact with the brethren.[36] This account, much coloured by legend, does not have the same substance as the previous episodes. However, it is no less full of interest. Note in particular the claim – albeit belated – by the two imprisoned missionaries to be Roman citizens. In this city, where people prided themselves on being among Romans,[37] and where the institutions were based on Roman models, the Christian evangelists felt at home. If they left Philippi, it was perhaps because people did not want them there any more,[38] but doubtless it was also because they wanted to resume the way to Rome, their real destination.

In fact, they left westwards by the Via Egnatia, leaving aside two important cities, Amphipolis, capital of the province of Macedonia Prima, and Apollonia, thirty miles further on, and went directly to Thessalonica, where there was a Jewish synagogue.[39] However, Thessalonica was also the provincial capital and the residence of the Roman governor. For Paul it was an important stage on his progress towards Italy. A church established in this great city could give him effective help towards this end. After preaching three successive sabbaths in the synagogue, Paul and Silas had gathered around them several Jews, many Greeks who sympathized with Judaism, and a certain number of women from local high society.[40] The leaders of the synagogue then stirred up street disorders and seized Jason, the host of Paul and Silas, and several other Christians. They handed them over to the authorities, accusing them of seditious behaviour. The Christians were released with a caution, but the situation had got so hot that the brethren sent the two missionaries to Beroea, an important place around forty miles west of Thessalonica, but away from the major roads. It also had a synagogue. Without giving up their long-term projects, the missionaries seized the occasion to preach to the Jews and the sympathizers who were meeting with them on the sabbath. They had real success, among both the Jews and the Greek sympathizers, and everything was going well when the leaders of the synagogue in Thessalonica, having got wind of Paul's activity in Beroea, hastened to the city and there stirred up popular agitation against him.[41] Paul had to decamp with great speed. He was escorted to the nearest port and taken to Athens by sea. There at least, almost 200 miles from Macedonia, he would be protected from the threats made against him in Thessalonica and Beroea. According to Acts 17.14, Silas and Timothy had remained in Beroea to continue the work that had been started, but Paul begged them to join him speedily in Athens. In his eyes the Macedonian chapter was closed and he needed all his colleagues to open a new mission field.

It is not that Paul had abandoned his relations with Macedonia and his young churches from the moment that he had to flee this region. A letter to the Philippians and two letters to the Thessalonians (one of which has sometimes been regarded as a letter to the Beroeans) attest the contrary. Moreover we know that Paul returned to Macedonia at least twice,[42] and wanted to do so more often,[43] that he sent very close colleagues to the Macedonian churches,[44] and that he had a particular affection for the Christians of Philippi.[45] These responded with very loyal financial support,[46] which a little later was to turn into the generous participation of the churches throughout Macedonia in the collection undertaken by Paul for the poor of Jerusalem.[47] It is not too much to say that for the apostle Macedonia had become a more important missionary base than southern Galatia, where he had found the first support for his enterprise of independent evangelization.

Despite the persistence of these very strong links with Macedonia, Paul's arrival in Achaea marks a turning point in his activity. Hitherto he had avoided the large Greek cities, because of the risk that they would occupy him for a long time and affect his progress towards Rome. What now delayed him in Athens, the intellectual capital of Hellenism? It was as if circumstances had suggested to him that, failing Rome, this great university centre to which people came from all over the empire to study could become his missionary base if he succeeded in creating an important church there. The account which Acts (17.15–34) gives us of Paul's evangelizing activity in Athens is unfortunately a very summary one, apart from the scene on the Areopagus, which has every appearance of being a literary composition aimed at emphasizing the speech in vv.22–31. This has been inserted by Luke in an arbitrary way. Moreover Paul's letters do not tell us anything about his relations with the Christians of this city. However, we learn enough in Acts 17 to know that Paul preached both in the synagogue, where the Jews were surrounded by sympathizers, and in the public arena. His preaching interested certain intellectuals, but he did not win many people over to the Christian faith. In short, his hope of establishing in Athens a large church aimed at serving as a counterbalance to Jerusalem and as a base for him was not realized. That doubtless explains why the apostle soon left for Corinth.

The Areopagus speech, sometimes attributed to the author of Luke-Acts, must certainly be seen as an example of the kind of preaching addressed by Christian missionaries in the last quarter of the first century to the purely pagan audiences which they encountered. The theology expressed in it is what the Hellenistic Jews stated in their missionary writings: a God who is creator, providence and judge, who rejects any representation of his person and who calls human beings to conversion, at a time when the Last Judgment is approaching. Despite a few echoes of Stoic ideas, all this keeps very close to biblical thought. However, the absence of any reference to sin and to human rebellion against God, and of any allusion to the cross, allows us to say that this is not a document which derives from the apostle Paul. What is being expressed here is the average thought of the Hellenistic churches of a later generation.[48]

In going from Athens to Corinth, fifty miles further west, Paul was leaving the intellectual centre of Hellenism, where he had at least met with a setback, to resume his journey towards Rome. In fact Corinth, which had been destroyed by the Roman army in 146 BCE, had been raised from its ruins a century later with the status of a Roman colony. Its exceptional geographical situation, at the crossroads of the land route between northern Greece and the Peloponnese and the sea route between the Adriatic and the Aegean seas, had led to the very rapid development of this new foundation, thanks to its commercial prosperity and the influx of a cosmopolitan population. Because of this, in 27 BCE the city was chosen as the capital of Achaea; it was the residence of the proconsul who administered this province. One could add that the city was very lively and famed for the loose morals of its inhabitants. Paul rediscovered in Corinth the Roman atmosphere which he loved, and could hope to benefit from the very close relations between the port and Italy. On his arrival in the city he made the acquaintance of a Jewish household which had been expelled from Rome some time earlier by a decree of the emperor Claudius which drove the Jews out of the capital (49 BCE). As these people, called Aquila and Priscilla, were tentmakers, just as he was, Paul joined them. On the sabbath he preached in the synagogue to a public made up of Jews and Greeks.

Since Silas and Timothy had rejoined him a little later with the money that they had collected in Macedonia, Paul could devote himself entirely to preaching and debate the messiahship of Jesus with the Jewish doctors. When he did not succeed in convincing them, the apostle broke with the synagogue and turned to the pagans. He had lodgings in the house of a certain Titius Justus, a non-Jewish sympathizer living alongside the synagogue. Paul's preaching was a great success, so much so that the leader of the synagogue, a certain Crispus, was baptized along with his family. It will be noted that these two figures had Latin names. In short, the church of Corinth was developing at full speed. Since the road to Rome remained barred by the decree of Claudius, the capital of Achaea served quite well as a missionary base for Paul and his companions. A nocturnal vision confirmed to the apostle that God wanted him to continue his preaching at Corinth and would protect his servant against all threats. This proved so true that Paul remained in the city for eighteen months, a far longer stay than any of his halts in previous cities.[49]

The leaders of the synagogue were increasingly hostile to the apostle's activity, so they tried to make the proconsul intervene. This man, a brother of the philosopher Seneca, was called Gallio; an inscription discovered at Delphi allows us to date his proconsulate in Achaea from the year 51–52 CE, or less probably from 52–53. He heard the accusation, which charged Paul with the crime of illegal religious propaganda, but would not give the defence even a hearing. He said that he had no competence to do so, since in his eyes Paul was still a Jew and this was an internal dispute within the Jewish synagogue. So the Christian community continued to benefit from the privileges granted to the Jews, whereas in fact it was no longer at all dependent on the synagogue authorities. Furious, the Corinthian Jews fell upon Sosthenes, the ruler of the synagogue, who was doubtless accused of being soft, and gave him a good thrashing right in front of the tribunal of the proconsul. But Gallio still refused to become involved. This attitude of the representative of Rome matched the wishes of Christians so closely that they noted it carefully.[50]

After this judicial episode, Paul remained for some time in Corinth, and then, doubtless thinking that the Corinthian church was sufficiently solid, he took leave of the brethren and embarked in the company of Aquila and Priscilla, not for Rome, but for Syria, going by Ephesus. This voyage, which is related only in Acts 18.18–23, remains most mysterious for us. Hardly has Paul left Corinth, in the nearby port of Cenchreae, than he has his head shaved after a vow.[51] This unexpected detail, which can hardly be said to be an apologetic invention on the part of the author, is difficult to interpret. The vow can only be a Nazirite vow, which carried with it the obligation not to cut one's hair until the object of the vow had been achieved.[52] But to what could this particular vow relate? Perhaps to a commitment not to return to Jerusalem and to Antioch until he had shown that the evangelization of the uncircumcised was indeed his affair.[53] Since Rome remained inaccessible because of the decree of Claudius, Paul could at least look back on the work accomplished over four years and feel freed from his vow. Furthermore, he left alone, since Aquila and Priscilla were not going beyond Ephesus. He refused to stop in this city to preach the gospel there, although the Jews of the city begged him to, and embarked immediately for Caesarea in Palestine. From there he visited the church (beyond question, the Jerusalem church). This move is reported in five words and by all accounts was fruitless, doubtless because the Jerusalemites were not ready to make the least concession to the schismatic who was trying to regain their favour. Paul then went to Antioch, apparently by land. Did he get a better reception there than in Jerusalem? That is not certain, although according to Acts 18.23 Paul 'spent some time there'. In short, he failed all along the line, and that explains the extreme reticence of the author of Acts.

Paul could only go back to the scenes of his former activity, to consolidate and develop his autonomous missionary work there.

7

Paul, Church Leader

Paul retraced from Antioch the journey which he had made some four years earlier, strengthening the disciples[1] in southern Galatia and Phrygia. From there he went down to Ephesus,[2] where some of his fellow workers, especially Aquila and Priscilla, had begun to evangelize the Jews, who already seem to have heard various echoes of the message of John the Baptist.[3] For three months Paul preached his gospel to the synagogue, and then, in the face of the vigorous opposition of a Jewish group, left this setting and began to teach every day in the school of a certain Tyrannos.[4] This lasted for two years,[5] and perhaps a bit longer.[6] He seems to have had considerable success and went far beyond the bounds of the city of Ephesus to exert influence over the whole of the province of Asia.[7] Here Paul's colleagues founded several churches around this time.[8] Unfortunately the Book of Acts gives us only vague information, tinged with legend, about the development of Paul's ministry in Ephesus.[9] However, it says enough to show that from then on Christianity was firmly established in Asia, beginning with the very large city which was its capital. Perhaps Paul had encountered violent opposition and run great risks in Ephesus,[10] where he was imprisoned several times by the Roman authorities.[11] Be this as it may, a major riot shook the city shortly before his departure,[12] directed against the monotheistic and iconoclastic propaganda of which Paul was one of the vehicles.

The undisputed leader of a group of missionaries which evangelized Asia during his stay in Ephesus, Paul had also recovered his authority over all the churches that he had founded over the previous years. This had not happened without some battles and disputes, as is shown by the letters written from Ephesus to some of these communities. While the Christians of Philippi, to whom one of these letters was sent, seem to have remained completely faithful to Paul, they were nevertheless cautioned against the 'dogs' who could have required them to be circumcised.[13] The situation was clearly less favourable in Corinth, where Paul's enemies and certain rivals had found ready ears while Paul was in Ephesus. With Apollos, a Jew from Alexandria armed with the biblical culture of this great centre of Hellenistic Judaism, and a preacher of a gospel in which a reference to Jesus was combined with influences from John the Baptist, things went quite well. Aquila and Priscilla, who had met Apollos at the synagogue in Ephesus during Paul's travels, had won him over to a more Pauline conception of the gospel,[14] and the church of Ephesus had commended him to the communities of Achaea, i.e. above all to the Corinthians. Apollos had been successful in Corinth, and this led some of the brethren to refer to him rather than to Paul.[15] In a letter to the church of Corinth, Paul censured this kind of declaration of allegiance and presented his ministry and that of Apollos as complementary: 'I planted, Apollos watered, but God gave the increase.'[16] So there does not seem to have been any conflict between the two missionaries, even if Apollos' knowledge and talents seem to have aroused the jealousy of Paul, who held firmly to his exclusive role as father of the Corinthian community.[17] We do not know the subsequent career of Apollos, who doubtless had already left Corinth when Paul wrote and did not desire to return there, despite Paul's encouragement.[18] It was Timothy, one of his most faithful colleagues, whom Paul sent to Corinth to remind the people there of his authority,[19] probably in the spring of 55. He was followed by Titus, who made several journeys to Corinth in 55 and 56 to represent Paul there.

The problem posed by the popularity of Apollos was far from being the only one in the life of the Corinthian church to preoccupy Paul. Everything indicates that Peter had also passed through this community and there had won the approval of a number of believers.[20] We do not know what attitude these people had to the rest of the church, in particular over common meals. But Paul does not seem too concerned about the influence of the person whom he almost always calls Cephas, a transcription of the Aramaic *Kepha*, perhaps in order to avoid suggesting for Peter the role of the rock on which the church is built which the Greek form of his name could indicate. He does not engage in any polemic against him, except in II Corinthians 10.12 and 11.15, where Peter is certainly meant but the adversary criticized remains anonymous. The tone becomes more lively when Paul attacks Judaizing missionaries who had challenged his apostolic authority and even his person before the Christians of Corinth. Were these colleagues of Peter, to whom Peter left it to attack Paul, or emissaries of James who were even more hostile? It is difficult to say. However, they aroused the indignation of Paul, who saw himself challenged on points in which his behaviour inspired some pride in him: his refusal to live at the expense of the community which he was in process of evangelizing;[21] his lack of eloquence and boldness;[22] his qualifications within Judaism;[23] his efforts to spread the gospel;[24] his personal revelations;[25] his very weaknesses.[26] In his fury Paul goes so far as to regard these people as frauds in the service of Satan,[27] while leaving the door open for forgiveness once the community has been freed from their grasp.[28] He even seems to have found these attacks so intolerable that he tried to put an end to them himself by making an unexpected journey to Corinth. This was not as successful as he had expected.[29]

The Corinthian church did not only suffer from the intrusion of Paul's rivals and adversaries. It was threatened by various tendencies connected with its pagan environment, its sociological composition,[30] and its lack of spiritual experience. These errors were primarily doctrinal. Some Christians, driven by an atmosphere dominated by the quest for wisdom, found the very sober preaching of the apostle quite inadequate and wanted to develop it into a philosophy. Paul does not deny that a wisdom should be offered to adult Christians,[31] but this is a wisdom relative to the secrets of God and revealed by the Spirit, which only the spiritual can understand. So what is envisaged here is the beginnings of a Christian doctrine, but in no way a kind of religious philosophy based on reason. This doctrine is not developed anywhere in Paul's correspondence with the Corinthians, unless it is in I Corinthians 15, where the apostle is forced to explain his ideas about the resurrection of the dead in order to dispel serious misunderstandings.

This theme, which is closely linked to that of the Last Judgment, took root in Jewish thought only at a late stage and continued to be challenged by the most conservative groups,[32] like the Sadducees. Not only did this eschatological picture inspired by Ezekiel 37 fit badly into the context of Hellenistic ideas about history, but it could seem outdated in the teaching of a Paul who put such a strong emphasis on the immediate and definitive acquittal of anyone who put his faith in Jesus Christ.[33] So we can understand how some Corinthians could have regarded salvation by faith as sufficient and the resurrection of the dead as a useless hypothesis. Paul energetically rejects this point of view, basing himself on the venerable tradition which referred to the resurrection of Christ and the appearances that had confirmed it.[34] These basic facts of the Christian faith absolutely exclude any denial of the resurrection of the dead, since the Risen Christ is 'the first fruits of those who are dead'[35] and opens up the way of resurrection to all who belong to him.[36] There remains the difficulty of the body in which this return to life is made; Paul responds to this by speaking of the spiritual body which at this moment takes the place of the animal body of both the dead and the living.[37] In short, it is the imagery of Ezekiel 37 that underlies the apostle's demonstration, but here it becomes a reasoned doctrine, stated in Greek terms far more abstract than those of the prophet of old.[38]

The Corinthian tendencies which Paul tries to correct are not only doctrinal. Detached from the Mosaic Law and the synagogue, the Christians of Corinth had to be inventive both in worship and in their moral behaviour. They asked the advice of their spiritual father on certain questions: virginity and marriage,[39] eating meat sacrificed to idols,[40] the hierarchy and use of the gifts of the Spirit.[41] Paul replied at great length, thus giving his correspondents directives which went well beyond the limits of the questions raised. On other subjects it is Paul who takes the initiative on the basis of information which he has received from certain members of the community. There are the case of a man who lives conjugally with his stepmother;[42] trials which set certain of the faithful against each other before pagan tribunals;[43] fornication with prostitutes;[44] disorder in community worship.[45] In all these cases the apostle expresses himself with authority and expects that the believers will put his advice and sometimes his orders into practice. What appears to us through these developments of Paul is a group with plenty of questions. Even if Jewish morality remains an occasional point of reference, the solutions that are being proposed are Christian, some based on words of Jesus and others dictated by the conviction that the end of time is near. Yet others are steeped in the experience of the Holy Spirit.

Particular attention needs to be paid to what the apostle says to the Corinthians about the Spirit.[46] On all the evidence Paul emphasized strongly that they should see this power from on high as the key to the new life to which the gospel called them. But while he was thinking above all of the existence of the community, the Corinthians had argued in individual terms and drew attention to the supernatural gifts which some of them enjoyed, deriving authority over their brothers and sisters from them: ecstatic forms of speaking, prophetic inspiration and healing gifts. The excessive individualism of these inspired figures made community life difficult and worship chaotic. So Paul tries[47] to extend the notion of inspiration as far as possible, emphasizing the diversity of the gifts of the Holy Spirit and the fact that all believers, even the most humble, belong to the same body of which they are the members, the body of Christ. This leads him to define the highest way which he wants all believers to take within the community: that of love. He gives a striking definition of this, asserting that it has an eternal value, like faith and hope, but that it is superior even to these two dimensions of spiritual life.[48] Finally, the apostle talks about the celebration of community worship. Here the Spirit must certainly blow, but order must be respected and the edification of participants must always be kept in mind. There is to be no speaking in ecstasy without interpretation and a preference must be shown for prophecy which is comprehensible rather than ecstatic speaking; only one person must speak at a time.[49] Two verses in this chapter add a prohibition against women speaking in assemblies;[50] this is in direct contradiction of I Corinthians 11.5 and, since it is inserted in two different places, depending on the manuscript, has every appearance of being a later addition. It seems to come from the milieu in which I Timothy was composed,[51] i.e. the next generation of the churches founded by Paul, which was much more conformist than the apostle and his contemporaries.

For all that, Paul is not a feminist. However, as the author of the formula 'there is no longer man nor woman',[52] he could not refuse women the right to prophesy or to pray in assemblies for worship. Still, he remained attached to a certain number of social conventions. Women had to have long hair and wear a veil, because they were subordinate to men, who had to have short hair and not wear veils. It was indecent for women to speak in worship without respecting these conditions.[53] In short, the Christian woman remained a woman, while having full rights to take part in the life of the church, the body of Christ. The concern for order which Paul emphasizes at this point, as with the interventions of inspired figures during worship, is repeated in the instructions which he gives to the Corinthians for celebrating the Lord's Supper.[54] Confronted with an unfortunate situation in which the Supper was regarded as a kind of free-for-all, without the community gathering round the Lord's table, Paul recalls the meaning of the tradition about the eucharist and the need for Christians to understand the sacred character of this meal. It requires of them a communal celebration, in memory of the death of the Lord Jesus.

The leader of a group of missionaries who all regarded him as their spiritual father and the inspired interpreter of the message of the gospel, Paul thus also appears to us, through the correspondence with Philippi and with Corinth, as the supreme authority recognized by a dozen local churches in Achaea, Macedonia, Asia and Galatia. Almost all of these had been founded by him, and their common characteristic was that they had burnt their bridges with the synagogues. For these communities coming to grips with the need to construct a morality, a community life and a cult, the apostle was both the witness to the earliest tradition, the spiritual father and the inspired bearer of the divine wisdom. At the cost of constant vigilance, he had succeeded in remaining their exclusive guide and spokesman. So we can understand that he wanted to use this powerful instrument to make good the failure of his solitary visit to Jerusalem in 52. He had been kept out of the way when he had presented himself alone to renew the links which had been broken in 48–49. So he hoped that if he arrived some years later at the head of a large delegation representing all the churches that he had founded, he would succeed in gaining a hearing from the leaders of the Jerusalem community. To give this delegation a concrete mission which would help to facilitate the conversations, he put forward the idea of a vast collection in the churches under him for 'the saints of Jerusalem who are in poverty'.[55] For many months Paul exhorted the churches related to him to show their generosity. He made practical suggestions, for example that each believer should set aside what he could spare during the week. He tried to urge on the laggards by mentioning the results achieved by other churches, and in the end of the day he seems to have had some success. Around autumn 57 everything was ready, and the delegation had been formed.[56]

At that very moment, Paul's situation had become difficult at Ephesus and throughout the province of Asia.[57] The apostle had come to the conclusion that he no longer had any scope for action around the circumference of the Aegean Sea.[58] So after becoming reconciled with the Jerusalem church, he wanted to leave for the West and reach Spain, stopping at Rome on the way. In short, he envisaged resuming the project that he had had to abandon around 50–51. He returned to Macedonia for some weeks and then went to spend the winter of 57–58 in Corinth. He left in time to go to celebrate the Passover in Philippi and immediately afterwards set off for Jerusalem, stopping at Troas, Miletus, Patara, Tyre, Ptolemias and Caesarea on the way.[59] He was at the head of a delegation of at least ten people representing all the churches that he had founded, for the most part pagan Christians, but also Jewish disciples like Timothy. Paul was no longer the isolated anti-establishment figure who had grasped his liberty ten years early, but the undisputed leader of a group of churches which had broken entirely with the synagogues and were leading an autonomous existence at the heart of pagan society.

We have only a very vague idea about the organization of these churches. Paul was clearly their head, and his colleagues went from one church to another to assert his authority and to maintain a certain doctrinal and disciplinary unity. But if we leave out the church of Philippi, which had *episcopoi* and deacons[60] whose precise functions are not clearly indicated, we do not know what ministries were exercised in these communities. Reading a text like I Corinthians 12–14, we get the impression that the spiritual gifts which many of the believers enjoyed gave them a cultic and moral authority among their brothers and sisters, without the functions being clearly defined. It was only after the demise of Paul and his chief colleagues that a church like that of Corinth was to give itself permanent ministers. The first letter of Clement of Rome, composed around 95 CE, speaks about these quite precisely. The letters to Timothy and Titus, which can be dated to around 80, attest both the persistence of a regional authority exercised by Paul's own companions and a consolidation of certain local ministries like those of *episcopoi*,[61] deacons[62] and elders.[63]

Paul's authority over these few churches which he founded is that of an apostle of Jesus Christ,[64] a title to which he was very attached,[65] though its precise significance was difficult to establish. In Paul's eyes it involved above all representing the Lord Jesus and carrying his gospel everywhere with an absolute authority. While he admits that he was the last to accede to this function,[66] he nevertheless claims all the rights attached to the title.[67] But if he yields nothing to his adversaries on this point in order to safeguard his authority over the communities, he also uses other arguments to make himself understood by the churches. The 'mercy of the Lord' has made him 'worthy of trust';[68] he hands on the commandments of the Lord;[69] he is inspired by God;[70] he is an example and has to be imitated;[71] he is the spiritual father of his correspondents, to whom he has been the first to bring the gospel.[72]

This last title is without doubt the main explanation of the extremely affectionate, even sentimental, tone that Paul uses to describe his relations with the Christians of the churches which he founded.[73] Far from being a vague term, the address 'brothers', which the apostle constantly uses in his letters, has a very strong sense. It expresses the solidity of the bonds created by the common faith. It will be noted that in giving the name 'churches', borrowed from the Deuteronomic tradition, to the local communities Paul claims for each of them the dignity of an assembly of God's chosen people which was at first reserved for the Jerusalem church. The links between the members of this people, founded in its very liberation, were necessarily very strong.[74] The emotional dimension of the common life and of the relationship between the apostle and the local churches appears very clearly in the account given in Acts of the journey of Paul and his delegation from Macedonia to Jerusalem.[75] Granted, this is a literary theme: the farewell of the man of God to those whom he has converted and his way to martyrdom. But some of the scenes which are described would seem authentic, and correspond well to what we know from the letters about the relations between the apostle and his churches. There is Paul's interminable sermon at Troas, before and after the celebration of the eucharist, throughout the night of the 'first day of the week', and hardly interrupted by the fall of one of his audience from the third floor. And there is the farewell speech given by the apostle to the elders of Ephesus when he is passing through Miletus. This speech recalls Paul's missionary work in Asia, pursued with perseverance despite all opposition; he announces that the journey to Jerusalem threatens to go wrong and that consequently he will not see his audience again; he exhorts them to pursue their ministry in the service of the flock by protecting it against attacks from outside and deviations within, not seeking to derive the least personal benefit from this activity.[76] His words, followed by prayer together, cause general emotion and make many tears flow. Even if this moving scene has quite a literary character, it is a good illustration of the atmosphere of the relations between Paul and the churches that he founded.

At the head of his imposing delegation, the apostle was received with some solemnity by the churches of Tyre, Ptolemais and Caesarea, which seem to have been the creations of the Hellenist missionaries driven from Jerusalem by the persecution following the lynching of Stephen. At Tyre and Caesarea, prophets announce to Paul that he will have grave difficulties in Jerusalem, but the apostle does not allow himself to be deterred and continues with his plan. In Jerusalem, or on the road to this city, a certain Mnason of Cyprus gives lodgings to the delegation before it meets with the leaders of the Jerusalem church.[77] Perhaps he was another Hellenist, showing how much the network created twenty-five years earlier in these regions by the members of this group who had been driven out of Jerusalem remained separate from the great church of the capital.

The delegation led by Paul was received by James, surrounded by all the elders, the day after it arrived.[78] Paul gave an account of the great success granted by God among the pagans through his activity, and those who heard him gave glory to God. It seemed that a negotiation could begin between the two groups, as in Galatians 2.1–10. However, according to Acts 21.20–25, an account which we have no cause to doubt, nothing of the sort happened. Paul was very firmly advised to go to the Temple with four brothers who were to purify themselves following a vow and to pay all their expenses – since he had arrived with full pockets. As for the fate of the pagans who had become believers, there was nothing to negotiate, since the Christian authorities in Jerusalem had already decided that they had to abstain from meat and pagan sacrifices, from blood and the meat of animals which had been strangled, and from immorality, and the notification of this decision had already taken place. In short, their intransigence was absolute. Paul tried to make dialogue possible by detaching himself from the delegation and doing the duty which had been imposed on him. He was lost, and his failure was total.

8

Paul, Theologian and Martyr

Since he had broken with the other Christian leaders in Antioch, Paul had been living under pressure, rushing from one place to another; seeking to plug the gaps which were forming in his preserve, namely the churches which he had founded; and trying to escape both the attacks of the synagogue and civic authorities and those of his Christian opponents. When he found time to dictate a letter it was to reply to questions which had been put to him, to defend himself against attacks, to prepare his action, in short to cope with urgent necessities. A certain number of the developments which feature in such letters had a doctrinal character, like some passages in the letter to the Galatians and the letters to the Thessalonians, or like I Corinthians 15 and II Corinthians 3. But these were teachings about particular points relating to the questions or needs of the church to which one or other of these letters was addressed.

Now during the years of his independent ministry Paul had many times encountered a situation which obliged him to innovate on the doctrinal level so that the believers could unite in a firmly knit community. The apostle was accustomed to using the podium which was offered to him by the synagogues in the cities which he visited, to preach his gospel there before Jews and sympathizers of pagan origin. However, by his intransigence and excesses of language, he had a way of alienating the leaders of these synagogues; they more or less rapidly excluded him from their community, along with those who had accepted his message.[1] Thus deprived of their natural framework, the Jews and persons of pagan origin who had attached themselves to Paul had no very evident reason to organize themselves into a new community. Some were used to living in conformity with the Mosaic Law; others accepted only certain commandments; yet others derived their rules of life from quite different sources. Confronted with this risk of dispersion, which drove Christianity towards a kind of sacramental self-service, very similar to the mystery religions which were so widespread in the Roman empire at this time, the apostle had been obliged to use doctrine as a basis for his exhortations to form a community uniting all believers. This need, which was felt from one city to the next, gradually gave rise to a kind of superior catechism which merely alluded to the essential articles of faith (one God, creator, legislator, providence and judge; Christ, Son of God, who died for the sins of the impious and was raised to give new life; the Holy Spirit, source of all kinds of gifts for the believers, etc.) and concentrated on two main ideas: acquittal in anticipation offered to every believer quite freely, and the need for a common life which would allow everyone to obey the divine will effectively through the action of the Holy Spirit within the group. The formation of a community was thus presented as the indispensable sequel to the individual acceptance of justification. By explaining these ideas to converts disorientated by the break with the synagogue and little inclined to unite because of their great diversity, wherever he went Paul succeeded in creating close-knit churches which did not need the framework of the synagogue to exist and develop.

This higher catechism doubtless remained oral over the years, for the simple reason that it was presented to believers by Paul himself some weeks or months after the beginning of his activity in a given place. It was only when, in the winter of 57–58, during his three-months' stay in Corinth,[2] Paul had time to reflect on the future of his missionary work, that the occasion arose for him to put this account in writing, in order to send it to the Christians of Rome. At that time the apostle turned what was still no more than an extended sketch into a letter, giving it a conventional introduction[3] and ending.[4] The main reason for this communication to the Romans, whom Paul did not know, was his desire to obtain their help for the work that he wanted to undertake in Spain, since he could not continue his activity in the eastern Mediterranean basin.[5]

However, there was doubtless a second reason, which politeness prevented Paul from stating openly and which justified his sending to the Romans the higher catechism aimed at convincing believers that they should organize themselves into a well-knit community. At this time the Christians of Rome do not seem to have been united in one church, and the apostle wanted to put an end to this situation in order to have more solid support in the capital. Since the expulsion of the Jews from Rome by Claudius in 49 CE, the passage of time and the replacement of Claudius by Nero had allowed the return of the numerous Jewish colony in the capital. This amounted to tens of thousands of people and had virtually no unity, since its members came from very different regions, were dispersed across the very large agglomeration, and met in several dozen synagogues. The Christian gospel, which had perhaps caused some tensions in the synagogues before 49,[6] had doubtless been brought to the capital at a very early stage by Jewish merchants and had remained confined to circles close to a certain number of these synagogues. So there must have been several Christian groups in Rome, closely linked to synagogues in various districts of the city, which had hardly anything to do with one another. We may in fact note that, contrary to his constant usage, Paul does not address his letter to 'the church of Rome' but 'to all the well beloved of God who are in Rome'.[7] He nowhere uses the term 'church' in the letter except in chapter 16,[8] and it is very uncertain whether this chapter belongs to the primitive text of the letter. It has also often been noted that the letter contains arguments addressed to Christians of Jewish origin, but also others which to all appearances are addressed to Christians of pagan origin. Since there is no indication of a clash between two groups at odds within the same community, we are led to suppose that the Roman Christians were dispersed into local groups in particular districts; their relationships with the nearest synagogue will have varied considerably and there will only have been occasional contacts between them.[9]

So it is to these Christians, who were scattered but relatively numerous and sufficiently influential to provide him with valuable help, that Paul addresses the fair copy of his higher catechism, with the carefully phrased remarks which can be noted above all in vv. 8–15 of the first chapter. As I have remarked, he does not take up the content of his initial preaching and the essential doctrinal themes of his message which he shares with other apostles. Rather, he dwells at length on questions on which he makes a more original personal contribution and which relate to the appropriation of the gospel rather than its content. Here we see him expressing his own thought with the aim of establishing an autonomous Christian church at a time when this objective was still far from being evident in the eyes of the disciples of Christ, who for the most part still felt very much at ease within Judaism.

The ideas expressed by Paul in the Letter to the Romans have had such an influence on later Christian thought, from Augustine to Karl Barth, that it is worth presenting them in broad outline,[10] while recalling that the first and second Christian centuries did not pay much attention to them. To understand the apostle's thought properly we must remember that he is writing about the destiny of humankind and not that of the individuals who make it up. Paul is arguing in collective terms and is speaking of the attitudes towards God adopted by human groups, except in 7.7–25, where he presents the impasse in which individual believers find themselves when seeking to obey God all by themselves. Thus in 1.18–3.20 the apostle paints a gripping picture of the moral degeneration of the pagan world; this is followed by a sharp attack on the self-satisfaction of Israel, whose failings are mercilessly emphasized. He ends this exposition with a catena of texts from the Psalms and the prophets showing that all, Jews and Greeks alike, are under the sway of sin. The existence of some virtuous pagans[11] and Jews[12] does not alter in any way this terrible statement, which dooms humanity to perdition. After a reminder of the traditional doctrine of the deliverance brought about by Jesus Christ for all those who accept this gift with faith,[13] Paul shows that a new people, that of the believers, has thus been created, with Abraham as its ancestor and salvation as its horizon.[14]

From 5.12 on, the apostle turns to the question of the life of believers in the long term. Just as Adam had doomed humanity to sin and death, so Jesus Christ has given it justice and life.[15] Dead with Christ in baptism, with him believers enjoy a new life which allows them a new obedience, the only one compatible with the justice received by faith.[16] But this obedience proves unattainable if one seeks it as an individual.[17] It is only by forming a community in which the Holy Spirit manifests itself in prayer and worship that believers find the supernatural strength to put themselves at God's disposal, to fulfil God's will and attain the certainty of the divine faithfulness.[18] So the formation of a local church is the key to Christian life. However, a major theological problem then arises. If a people inspired by the Holy Spirit is formed through the grace given in Jesus Christ, what about the historical Israel? Is its mission finished? Has it been rejected by God? Paul devotes a long section to this question, which is very important for him (chapters 9–11). Without following the ins and outs of his argument, one can at least say that the apostle resolutely dismisses the idea of a rejection of Israel by God. The hardening towards the gospel on the part of a large number of Jews is meant to allow the pagans to have access to salvation before the divine mercy finally triumphs over the disobedience of Israel, whose election is irrevocable. Having thus set the new people of God over against Israel, Paul then launches on a long exhortation to a community life which will be a true offering to God.[19] Particular emphasis is put on the need for tolerance between brethren who have different practices, and on the acceptance by the 'strong' of certain limitations on

their freedom in order to help the 'weak', to whom their conscience
dictates certain abstinences or observances. In short, in order to allow
the co-existence within the same church of very different people, each
individual must make an effort, without ever imposing his own convictions or customs on others. That will make community life all the
richer and more solid.[20]

Unfortunately we do not know whether the Christians of Rome
heeded Paul's advice and united in a church which practised a large
degree of tolerance among its members. Acts 28, which describes the
apostle's activity in Rome, does not allow us to give a clear answer to
this question. However, it does give the impression of the absence of any
church structure in the capital, even if some of the brethren have been
to meet the apostle and his companions.[21] In fact Paul only addresses
Jews of note on his arrival in order to present his case.[22] Besides, we do
know that the Roman Christians were still very divided some years
later, at the time of Paul's martyrdom.[23] So we may suppose that it was
only after they had undergone the terrible trial of Nero's persecution in
64 CE that the Christians of the capital gradually found the way to
unity and formed a well organized church which from before the end of
the first century exercised real authority over other communities.

Whatever the effect produced in Rome by Paul's letter, we have some
reason to suppose that the apostle, satisfied with having set down in
writing his higher catechism, himself had several copies of his letter
made, first of all for the various Christians in Rome, but also for
other recipients. Some manuscripts have in fact dropped the two
mentions of Rome in the letter,[24] transforming this document into a
kind of encyclical addressed to all Christians. Furthermore, the end of
the letter presents some textual oddities which suggest that the whole of
chapter 16 is a later addition. It has sometimes been suggested that the
very numerous salutations contained in this chapter are a compilation
of salutations added at the end of several copies of the letter, or salutations intended for the church of Ephesus, which Paul had left some
weeks earlier and to which he could have wanted to sent a copy of his
higher catechism. Be this as it may, nothing allows us to suppose that
the impressive exposition of Paul's own thought in Romans 1–15 would
have had any particular influence outside the small circle of his children
in the faith.

Some months after presenting his personal ideas on Christian life to
the Christians of Rome, Paul had had no possibility of holding conversations with the leaders of the Jerusalem church. Immediately after his

arrival these had asked him to show his fidelity to Judaism, separating him from his delegation of representatives of churches which he had founded in order to do so. He yielded to their demands and went to the Temple, there to perform the rites required of him. Some Jews from Asia, on recognizing Paul, denounced him to the crowd as a profaner of the sanctuary and thus sparked off a riot. Paul was seized and would have been lynched had not the tribune of the Roman cohort on guard sent in his troops; these took hold of the apostle and led him, not without some difficulty, to the fortress Antonia, where this unit was garrisoned.[25] Even if several elements in the accounts of Acts 22 and 23 pose problems, notably the two speeches of Paul reported there, there is hardly any doubt that that the apostle, under great threat from the Jewish side, remained imprisoned in the fortress Antonia until his transfer to Caesarea. Without being accused of the least crime, he was thus out of action as far as achieving his mission to the church of Jerusalem or resuming his ministry elsewhere was concerned. He was in fact to remain a prisoner until the end of his days. Separated from his churches and the majority of his companions and fellow-workers, he thus entered on a new phase of his existence.

Paul's transfer to the Roman governor at Caesarea further distanced him from the Jerusalem church, and there is nothing to suggest that it tried to maintain contact with this burdensome figure. Doubtless the majority of the members of his delegation returned home crestfallen, in company with some of the apostle's fellow-workers, leaving only some people authorized to take care of Paul in his prison. The money collected for the poor in Jerusalem will have served over the following years to pay the expenses of Paul and his companions.

The governor Felix refused to judge Paul's case and kept Paul in prison until the end of his mandate in Palestine (60 CE). When Felix's successor, Porcius Festus, seemed more disposed to yield to pressure from the Jewish authorities, the apostle demanded to be judged in Rome by the emperor. The governor allowed this immediately, all too happy to be rid of this difficult case. After giving Paul a last occasion to bear witness at length to his faith before King Agrippa II and his sister Berenice, the future mistress of Titus,[26] the author of Acts recounts in great detail Paul's journey under guard from Caesarea to Rome.[27] This account, the most polished part of the work, is all to the glory of the apostle, who shows himself calm and authoritative in the most dramatic circumstances, beginning with the shipwreck of his vessel off the island of Malta. Despite this bias and the probable imitation of a literary model, this passage remains a valuable document about the techniques and the vicissitudes of sailing out of season in this period, and also about the biography of Paul, who had already been ship-wrecked three times.[28] He was long hardened to danger in all its form. Despite the difficult situations in which he finds himself, the apostle is presented as a witness who grasps every occasion to express or defend his faith. Finally Paul's arrival and installation in Rome are reported.[29] Despite a warm welcome from certain Christian brothers,[30] the apostle cannot be integrated into any community there, since he is under house arrest and constantly guarded by a soldier. After an attempt to bear witness to the Jews, in which he does not gain their general acceptance, Paul is thus limited to receiving visitors and bearing witness to them. The author does not tell us whether he won many of them over to the faith.[31]

This situation lasted for two years, i.e. into the year 63 CE. The Acts of the Apostles stops there, without giving any indication whether Paul's trial before the imperial tribunal took place at the end of this period or whether the apostle was freed, since his Jewish adversaries from Jerusalem had not shown up. For want of sufficiently effective support from the Christians of Rome, still split up into several groups, it is in any case improbable that the apostle set in motion his plan to evangelize Spain. Certainly the first letter of Clement of Rome, com-posed around 95 CE,[32] says that Paul went 'to the limits of the West', but there is nothing to back up this rhetorical formula. The Acts of Peter, a very legendary text composed about 180, speaks of Paul's mission to Spain, but it has no historical value.[33] Attempts have been made to use certain facts in the letters to Timothy and Titus to demonstrate that on the contrary Paul left Rome for the East, to visit all the churches which he had founded, that he was arrested and returned to Rome under guard, was again tried, and finally executed around 67. Such a reconstruction of the last years of the apostle seems very fragile.[34] In fact, it is more probable that Paul's trial took place in 63, that it ended with a death sentence, doubtless for subversion, and that the apostle was executed shortly afterwards. That is, unless he perished in 64 in the great persecution launched against the Roman Christians after the burning of Rome. Be this as it may, Paul will have died in 63 or 64, without having been able to leave the capital and without having succeeded in uniting the Roman Christians as he had hoped to.

In short, the last five or six years of Paul's life were a period of trials which were all the more painful since this active evangelist and head of a church who was very attached to his flock had been reduced to almost total impotence, both in Jerusalem and in Caesarea and Rome. Moreover, abandoned as he was to his fate by the Jerusalem church, cut off from the churches which he had founded, and badly supported by the Christians of Rome who remained very divided, he had only a few faithful colleagues around him. Whatever may have been the circumstances of his death, he perished at the hands of the Roman power, whereas he had always relied on Rome and its representatives to facilitate the spread of the gospel. The martyrdom of this marginalized figure made hardly any mark on the Roman Christians, even if at the end of the first century Clement of Rome draws a parallel between his death and that of Peter,[35] and various apocrypha from the end of the second century relate Paul's death, mentioning the existence of his tomb on the road to Ostia. It was only in the fourth century that for Romans Paul became the counterpart of Peter, in both literature and Christian art.

So we may say that the apostle to the Gentiles ended his life and his ministry in quite wretched conditions. The few local churches which he founded risked being taken over by representatives of other Christian tendencies. His letters, filed in the archives of the communities to which they were addressed, were unknown to almost all Christians. His feverish existence and vigorous thought ended up in a failure which was apparently irredeemable. As other branches of the Christian movement were undergoing a very serious crisis at the same time, the future of Christianity could have appeared dark.

9

The Great Crisis of the 60s

At the beginning of the 60s CE, the Christian church was a group of modest size, but impelled by real dynamism and quite firmly organized around its centre, the city of Jerusalem. Within the Judaism of this time it formed a small and ardent minority which, under the direction of a prestigious leader, James, brother of the Lord, regarded itself as the prefiguration of the eschatological assembly of the chosen people. During the pilgrimages which marked the festivals of the Jewish calendar, this church brought together numerous pilgrims who had come to believe in Jesus Christ and commemorated with them the Master's passion. It had a real influence on Jewish opinion and James, its head, enjoyed considerable prestige among the people by reason of his exemplary piety. The Christian churches of the Diaspora accorded him a complete doctrinal and disciplinary primacy. The Christian mission to synagogues dispersed throughout the world, under the leadership of Peter, one of the first disciples of Jesus, accepted the authority of the Jerusalem church and conformed to the rules and impulses which came from the leaders of this centre.

Certainly, some differences came to disturb this well-ordered picture, but they remained such a minority feature that their existence did not constitute a very important problem. The Hellenists, who had broken with Jerusalem a quarter of a century earlier, still existed in numerous places on the Syro-Phoenician coast, but they seem to have lost much of their initial verve because they had not clearly opted for the evangeliza-tion of the pagans, while their opposition to the Temple isolated them from the majority of Jews. The churches founded by Paul had been crippled by the imprisonment and then the death of their apostle. Grouped around the Aegean, cut off from the synagogues in the cities where they had been established, rejected by the mother church of Jerusalem, they were capable only of continuing to show loyalty to their founder. They no longer carried much weight in the Christian movement as a whole. One could even suppose that, under the pressure of the

Christian majority, they would end up accepting views less radical than those of Paul.

A series of dramatic events was to shake this fine edifice which, round about the same time, seemed to have been consolidated by the neutralization and subsequent death of Paul, who posed the great challenge to it. The first of these episodes was the murder of James, the linchpin of the whole edifice, in 62 CE.[1] We have two accounts of this event, as I remarked earlier. They differ considerably. The later and more legendary one goes back to Hegesippus, a Palestinian Christian writing around 175 CE; his *Memoirs* are quoted by Eusebius in his *Church History*, composed at the beginning of the fourth century.[2] He puts the martyrdom of James shortly before the siege of Jerusalem by the Roman army in 69 and makes it a lynching organized by the 'scribes and Pharisees', jealous of the success of James' preaching to the Jews. The account is confused and quite improbable, but some details in it could be historical. The other narrative is that of Flavius Josephus,[3] which goes back to the end of the first century and seems closer to historical reality. According to Josephus, the high priest Hanan took advantage of the death of the procurator Festus (62) and the delay of his successor, Albinus, who only arrived in Palestine several months afterwards, to convene the Sanhedrin. He brought before it several persons accused of having violated the Law, including James; they were condemned and subsequently stoned. Later Hanan was dismissed from his post as high priest as a result of the scandal caused by this affair. Here James is much less at the centre of the drama and it is not even certain whether the others to be condemned were Christians. This is the account to be preferred.

Whatever may have been the precise circumstances of James' martyrdom, it was a harsh blow to a church which derived much of its prestige from the presence at its head of a figure very close to Jesus and renowned for his great piety. An attempt was made to maintain the institution by electing in place of James a certain Symeon, son of Clopas, uncle of Jesus,[4] but this kinsman of the Lord never had the same authority as his predecessor. Despite the legendary details which Eusebius gives about his martyrdom, again according to Hegesippus,[5] we have no idea of how he exercised his ministry, which would have lasted until the reign of Trajan, i.e. to the beginning of the second century. Since a parallel tradition, also reported by Eusebius according to Hegesippus,[6] relates that two grandsons of Jude, brother of Jesus, who ruled the churches – and even 'all the church' – until the reign of Trajan, appeared before the emperor Domitian (81–96) and barely escaped death, we must perhaps imagine a kind of collective episcopate exercised by the kinsfolk of Jesus towards the end of the first century. Moreover this monopolization of ecclesiastical power by the family of Jesus seems to have aroused some opposition within the church itself.[7] It is the sign of a power under challenge, which no longer had the undivided authority of a James. Doubtless the Jerusalem church was no longer the beacon illuminating all the communities that it had been before 62.

This diminution in the centralizing influence of Jerusalem is easily explained by other factors than the lack of striking personalities to succeed James and the dogmatic disputes which seem to have divided the church after his demise.[8] In fact from 66 on, Jewish Palestine was caught up in the maelstrom of the revolt against Rome and the very brutal repression that it set off. As we know, this ended in the fall of Jerusalem and the destruction of the Temple in 70. These tragic events were accompanied by very violent upheavals and conflicts within Palestinian Judaism, which had increasingly been taken over by the Zealot party, particularly in Jerusalem. We know virtually nothing about the position adopted by the Christians towards the Jewish revolt and the seizure of power in the capital by the Zealots. If the murder of Zechariah son of Barachiah mentioned in Matthew 23.35 is that of Zechariah son of Baruch, one of the leaders of the peace party in Jerusalem in 70, as some critics think, it could be said that the Christians of the capital disapproved of this action by the Zealots and therefore did not join them.[9] Moreover Eusebius[10] reports that the Jerusalem church left the capital before the siege, without dating this event precisely. He adds that the Christians from Jerusalem took refuge in Pella, a city of Transjordan populated by pagans. This exodus has been put in question by a number of critics, who find Eusebius' account improbable. It must be conceded that at the least it is a simplification of a complex reality. However, we must avoid succumbing to hyper-criticism here. There is nothing improbable about the flight of the church leaders to Pella, since this city remained outside the war. Other members of the church doubtless took refuge in other localities, while remaining in contact with their spiritual leaders established at Pella. Yet others, perhaps quite a large number, remained in Jerusalem, there to take part in the struggle against the Romans. However, we cannot say whether these splits followed existing doctrinal divisions. Be this as it may, we can easily imagine the violence of the opposition aroused by such different choices.

Once the war was over the survivors surely had some difficulty in being reconciled with one another. Since Jerusalem had not been entirely destroyed, it is probable that the refugees settled there again little by little, the Christians as well as the others. Eusebius[11] says that up to the siege of the city by Hadrian in 135 there was a great church in Jerusalem, which presupposes the existence of quite a large community. But we know nothing of the life of this group, and it is evident that it no longer had any authority over the churches of the Diaspora. The death of James, the hesitations over his succession, and the terrible upheaval of the Jewish war and its consequences, such as the end of pilgrimages, had undermined the dominant position of the Jerusalem church. From a quasi-papal system, the Christian churches had passed directly to a congregationalist regime, based on the local communities and the relations that these wanted to establish with one another.

The apostle Peter, who in the 50s and 60s had made been the leader of the missionary enterprise in communion with Jerusalem, could have concentrated some power in his hands at this time. But he too had been martyred before the end of the 60s and had no successor of the same stature. I mentioned above how large his missionary field had been.[12] An apostle who, like him, could write or have written a letter to Christians of five Roman provinces forming more than three-quarters of Anatolia[13] could have worked towards some kind of federation, even after the disappearance of Jerusalem as a centre. He would have had all the more chances of success since his message as presented in I Peter has no striking features nor any originality; it puts all the emphasis on the integration of Christians into the surrounding society. However, as chance would have it, the apostle Peter did not survive the upheavals of the 60s CE. While we do not know in what circumstances he went to Rome, nor whether his martyrdom took place very soon after his arrival, we can at least say that various indications converge to suggest that he was executed in the capital of the empire.[14] This execution, which legend has described in impressive terms, is known to us only through texts which are difficult to interpret and through very imprecise archaeological traces. It could have taken place at the time of the massacre of Christians ordered by Nero after the burning of Rome in 64,[15] but that remains uncertain. While accepting that the date of 64 CE is thus the most probable for Peter's martyrdom, I would leave open the possibility of a later date. The Christians of Rome, who had still been split into a number of groups some years earlier, as we have seen, could have gained an authority over all the churches of the Roman empire after the destruction of Jerusalem by rallying behind a prestigious leader like Paul or Peter. However, such a process, which took place later, was prevented around 70 CE not only by the death of the two apostles in question but also by the terrible trial of the Neronian persecution.

The fire which ravaged Rome in July 64 caused such damage and was accompanied by so many rumours that Nero had to find culprits. These were the Christians, but for what reason we do not know. After a hasty trial a large number of them were condemned to death and then executed collectively in scenes of frightful cruelty. Tacitus, who reports these events[16] and had no particular sympathy for this bizarre sect, could not help feeling sorry for the poor people, victims of an unscrupulous despot. It is easy to imagine the terrible shock suffered by the surviving Roman Christians. It certainly took them many years to get over this disaster, for which nothing had prepared them. So it is not surprising that they were not in a position to play a role in federating the churches after the fall of Jerusalem.

Traditional historiography has long accepted, following Tertullian, a Christian author from the end of the second and beginning of the third centuries, that after the mass executions inflicted on the Christians of Rome, the imperial power had outlawed Christianity throughout the Roman empire by an *Institutum neronianum* which made membership of the church alone punishable by death. The existence of such a decree is highly improbable, although Tertullian mentions it in his *Apologia*. What changed in relations between Christianity and the Roman empire following the persecution of the Christians of Rome by Nero was that the imperial authorities began to make a distinction between Jews and Christians. Thus the status of Judaism as a *religio licita* progressively ceased to protect the Christians, who were therefore delivered over to the whims of the police and the administration by virtue of the power of *coercitio* which allowed them to act to maintain public order. But there is nothing to suggest that the persecution of 64 extended to other regions, or that the Christians were the object of a systematic repression before the beginning of the third century. For a long time there were still only localized persecutions, which came about more or less accidentally.

Thus around 70, the Christian churches had successively lost the three protagonists of the first generation, James, Peter and Paul, and it was difficult to find successors. The Christians of Rome, still badly organized and decimated by the Neronian persecution, had the greatest difficulty in getting over this trial. Moreover this had detrimental consequences for all the churches of the empire, since from now on they were more exposed to authoritarian measures provoked by local circumstances or the ill-humour of particular administrators. The churches of Palestine had been ravaged by the Jewish War, and the Jerusalem church had lost its influence over all the Christian communities, who from now on lacked any co-ordination.

However, the upheaval undergone by the small Christian group was nothing to that experienced by Judaism. The destruction of the Temple, which had resulted in the cessation of sacrificial worship and pilgrimages, was a disaster as serious as the worst catastrophes in the history of Israel. The whole equilibrium of Jewish religion was put in question, and the risk of a definitive dispersal of the synagogues became real. For the Christian churches, almost all of which still leaned on the synagogues, this was an additional danger – or perhaps, as we shall see, an opportunity to be grasped for convincing more Jews of the messiahship of Jesus.

The danger of dissolution into its surroundings which threatened a Judaism deprived of its Temple was very quickly combated, thanks to the initiatives taken by an old Pharisaic rabbi from Jerusalem, Johanan ben Zakkai. The life of this figure is surrounded by legends prompted by the importance of his role in Jewish history. After a long career in Jerusalem, Johanan ben Zakkai found himself trapped in the city besieged by the Roman army, although he was totally opposed to the armed rebellion against Rome. He escaped the city in a shroud, pretending to be dead. When he arrived in the Roman camp he asked as a favour to be allowed to establish a rabbinic school in the occupied territories in which he could teach his doctrine; this attached great importance to obedience to the civil authorities. He was to settle at Jamnia, a place about twenty-five miles west of Jerusalem, in the coastal plain. His school was a great success; it sought to give Judaism a new religious centre,[17] somewhat later creating a new Sanhedrin and claiming some of the powers formerly held by the high priest of Jerusalem, in particular that to fix the calendar. Since Johanan ben Zakkai was a Pharisee, it was Pharisaic ideas that were presented to the synagogues through this channel, and over a quarter of a century they found an increasingly favourable welcome in them. As other parties of Palestinian Judaism had been destroyed by the Jewish war (the Sadducees, Zealots and Essenes), it was a Pharisaic form of Jewish religion that became established everywhere. The best indication of this is that in the last years of the first century CE, Patriarch Gamaliel II, the head of the

Jamnia Sanhedrin, was able to convene an assembly representing the whole of Judaism. At it the list of books belonging to the biblical canon was fixed and to the twelfth of the Eighteen Benedictions recited in the synagogue was added a phrase cursing the *minim* (= heretics) and perhaps also the Nazarenes. By virtue of this, the Christians who remained members of synagogues were obliged to leave them; moreover, if we are to believe the Fourth Gospel, the synagogues had begun to exclude the supporters of Jesus Christ.[18]

We shall be returning to the break between Judaism and Christianity which such decisions made inevitable.[19] However, it can be said here that the Pharisaic reform thus offered to Judaism doubtless saved it from disintegration and dissolution into the surrounding world, though at the cost of some impoverishment. The rich diversity of Judaism prior to 70, both in Palestine and in the Diaspora, was soon removed to make way for what has to be called an orthodoxy, even if in Judaism this term does not have such intellectual connotations as it does in Christianity. The crisis provoked by the destruction of the Temple was so serious that this step had to be taken to save Judaism. Subsequent history confirms this, since from the Mishnah to the Talmud it was the choices made by the school of Jamnia in the last thirty years of the first century that were the basis for the formation of rabbinic Judaism as it still exists today.

10

The Christian Counter-Offensive

Since the progressive reconstruction of a Judaism unified around Pharisaic practices took more than a generation, it would be naive to believe that between 70 and 100 CE the Christian communities, which were themselves completely dispersed, all had the same relations with the synagogues and experienced the same problems in the places where they had been established. We may leave on one side the communities of Pauline origin, which were already completely independent from Jewish institutions. Among the other local churches which remained more or less within the synagogues, like many other groups of *minim*, situations varied considerably, depending on the dominant tendency of the nearest synagogue and the ways in which it followed the reform being carried out by the teachers of Jamnia. They also varied depending on the theological colouring of each church. In short, it is difficult to present a synthesis of a diverse reality which is not at all well known, for lack of any documents.

However, with the help of sparse texts which illustrate these situations, we can analyse some cases which allow us to get a general idea of the relations with Judaism experienced by the Christian generation between 70 and 100, from Rome to the Euphrates and from Pontus to Egypt. The profound disarray of the Jews in the face of the disaster which had struck them left many of them very weak when it came to defending their traditional faith. The resistance which the great majority of them had offered to Christian affirmations diminished. Some Christians evidently became aware of this, and could have hoped that the gospel was going to appeal to those who had hitherto rejected it. They only had to plead their cause in slightly new terms, and they would get over obstacles which had hitherto been insuperable, taking advantage of the shaking of many Jewish certainties.

The Letter of James illustrates a first way of approaching this problem.[1] This brief writing, composed in good-quality Greek, is certainly not the work of the brother of the Lord; there is nothing to suggest that he knew that language so well. The most probable hypothesis is that it dates from about 80 CE. The place of its composition is totally unknown, though scholars have sometimes envisaged a Greek-speaking city in Palestine like Caesarea or Tiberias. The author calls himself 'James, servant of God and of the Lord Jesus Christ'. This might seem quite neutral, but he expresses himself with an authority which irresistibly suggests the 'brother of the Lord', head of the Jerusalem church until 62. So this is a pseudonymous work which appeals to the great figure, who well after his death remained the supreme point of reference for all Jewish Christians. Those to whom it is addressed are designated by the expression 'the twelve tribes which live in the Diaspora'; this immediately suggests Jewish, or at least Jewish-Christian, recipients. Incidentally, the word recipients is inappropriate for the readers envisaged by this writing. It is, rather, an encyclical addressed to all the Jews of the Diaspora, including Jewish Christians, by a Christian writer who is assuming the authority of James, a figure known for his piety and his fidelity to the Mosaic Law. The author treats his readers as 'brothers', which suggests that, good Jew as he is, he feels close to them. Scholars have even gone so far as to say that the letter is a Jewish document, barely Christianized by two mentions of the 'Lord Jesus Christ'.[2] This thesis is excessive, since there are numerous indications that the writing is Christian – for example the debate on salvation by faith or by works,[3] which presupposes a certain knowledge of the thought of the apostle Paul. But if the author certainly expresses himself as a Christian, he does so with extreme discretion, as if to avoid causing any offence.

It has sometimes been argued that the letter of James has no plan, like the literary model of Hellenistic exhortations, which are deliberately disordered so that each piece of advice or reminder is received for itself and not as an element of an argument or a larger whole. Certainly the style of this writing resembles the charming disorder of Hellenistic exhortations. However, at the centre of the letter there is a group of instructions which show a real unity: 2.1–3.18. It has often been noted that 2.14–26 attacks the Pauline doctrine of salvation by faith. It would be more correct to say that the author is criticizing an insipid form of Paul's thought which neglects what follows the apostle's affirmation of salvation by faith, namely the call to bear the fruits of the Spirit. In short, the author of the Letter of James is not referring to the letters of Paul, which he had not read, but to the life of the churches which had inherited Paul's message, as he believed that he could observe it from the outside. These churches, cut off from the synagogues and totally detached from the Mosaic Law, seemed to him to be lost in the depths of the Hellenistic world and the mystery religions, which made no connection between religious faith and moral life. Moreover it could be that this charge was not undeserved, at least in certain quarters. Why this attack on the Christian minority which arose out of Paul's activity and formed communities independent of the synagogues? Perhaps the writer was seeking to dissociate himself from some burdensome brothers at a time when he wanted to win the Jews over to the gospel.

The passages which surround the section I have just mentioned[4] confirm this analysis. In them the author vigorously criticizes church practices bound up with the celebration of worship independently of the synagogue assemblies. The first of these developments attacks in lively terms the respect shown to the rich by certain communities. To all appearances the author has a profound mistrust of wealth and the wealthy. He severely condemns communities in which the rich have been given a privileged place and calls on them to show greater ethical seriousness, referring to the Law of Moses. We may ask whether the attack is not also directed at the churches which inherited Paul's missionary work. In fact, in his quest for independence from the synagogues, Paul had deliberately relied on people of high social rank who also had substantial means, since these could hold Christian assemblies in their vast dwellings and provide financial support for the new communities. This tendency to cultivate the rich and make use of their resources to facilitate the life of the church doubtless continued after the demise of the apostle. It would have remained one of the distinctive features of the Pauline communities. The author, who wants to show the need to mistrust riches,[5] is anxious to distance himself from brothers known for their indulgence towards the rich. On this point, too, he dissociates himself from the Pauline churches in order to be able to present his ideas better to all the Jews of the Diaspora.

The intention is the same in James 3.1–18. It has not always been noted that this passage is merely the development of the idea expressed in 3.1, namely that in an assembly it is not possible for everyone to want to teach. The author, accustomed to the rules of the synagogues, finds it intolerable and dangerous that anyone whatsoever can speak in order to teach the brethren. He cannot bear the disorder of the charismatic meetings and he mistrusts the uncontrollable effusions of the inspired, which are a combination of good and bad. Only brothers who have attained wisdom should be authorized to speak. They are also the ones who will bring about peace in the community. Here the author is attacking communities which have arisen out of the activity of Paul and his group, in which worship doubtless continued to take place in a very disordered way, as in I Corinthians 14.This amazed and scandalized the Jews and Jewish Christians.

These second and third chapters of the Letter of James thus form a section at the heart of the work criticizing the life and doctrine of the churches of Pauline origin. For all the Jews who knew them, these churches, remote from the synagogues and somewhat fixed in the habits that they developed at the beginning, were an insurmountable obstacle to accepting the gospel. The author of the letter wants to show that these communities are marginal and that the great majority of Christians have nothing to do with them. So his message does not depend on the errors of some misguided brothers. There is nothing to stop it being presented to all the Jews of the Diaspora. This message gives only a very limited place to christology. The doctrine of God is mentioned in several places;[6] there is nothing very original about it, even if some neatly turned phrases appear in these passages. It is an entirely Jewish conception of God. The Holy Spirit is not mentioned anywhere. In this framework, which is very familiar to Jewish readers, the author is above all preoccupied with giving moral and spiritual advice and exhortations. These refer sometimes to the Law,[7] and sometimes to the words of Jesus (there are numerous allusions to the Sermon on the Mount). As I have already remarked, the most striking feature of this ethical teaching is the severity shown towards the rich and the favouring of poverty.

Is it rash in these conditions to see the letter of James as an attempt to present the Christian message as the most perfect form of Judaism, addressed to the Greek-speaking Diaspora, at a time when the Pharisaic reform had not yet made much progress and the synagogues were still engaged in seeking a way which would allow them to live out their faith without Temple worship and without pilgrimages? There is nothing to indicate that this attempt met with the least success, but the curious document that is the Letter of James doubtless shows us an attitude which was making great headway among the Christian majority during the ten to fifteen years which followed the destruction of the Temple.

The Gospel of Matthew is another indication of the combativeness of the Christian majority in seeking to win over the Greek-speaking synagogues to Christianity before the final triumph of the school of Jamnia.[8] As with the letter of James, the geographical origin of this Gospel is uncertain. Scholars sometimes think of Syria or Phoenicia, regions where there were many Jews and where the use of Greek was quite widespread, above all in the cities. However, the work does not aim to respond to regional problems. The public envisaged is the whole of the Greek-speaking Diaspora, whether it had already accepted the Christian message or remained opposed to it. The generally accepted date is around 90–95 CE. The author is faced with synagogues which have increasingly been taken in hand by the Pharisaic reformers. However, he continues to hope that he will win a large number of the members of these synagogues over to the gospel, in particular those whom the new orthodoxy deterred. Like the author of the Letter of James, he presents Christianity to them as the profoundest form of Judaism for the period when the Temple has disappeared. But he parts company with him totally over christology. Instead of passing over christology almost completely, so as not to provoke negative reactions on the part of Jews, he emphasizes it throughout his work. In his eyes it is the heart of authentic Judaism and would not be an obstacle to the adherence of honest members of the synagogues.

However, because of the considerable progress made by the Pharisaic reform, the appeal addressed to the mass of faithful Jews necessarily entailed a vigorous polemic against the new rulers of the synagogues. As we know, the Gospel of Matthew is very hard on 'the scribes and Pharisees, hypocrites'. Chapter 23 in particular is a collection of extremely lively attacks on the groups carrying out the reform. The evangelist focusses his attack on what in his view is the yawning abyss between their teaching, which is very rigorous, and their behaviour, which tends towards dishonourable compromises. However, beyond this violent polemic there is a basic difference between the Christians on one side and the scribes and Pharisees on the other. The evangelist does not approve of an accommodating hermeneutic which makes it possible to apply the commandments to the letter in ordinary life, but he recommends a radical interpretation. Since these rules of life are the expression of the will of God, they are to be understood in the absolute sense which alone befits the divine presence. The way in which the evangelist reads commandments of the Decalogue quoted in Matthew 5.17–48 turns these rules intended to organize social life into calls to personal heroism, the only appropriate behaviour when the believer is facing God. Confronted with a Pharisaic movement entirely devoted to making the Law quite precise in order to adapt it to all concrete situations, the Jesus of Matthew gives this same Law the function of a waymark along the route which leads to God. In other words, faced with a well-defined and well-organized synagogue, he does not counter it with an alternative group which is even more solid, but with an ambitious missionary programme (chapter 10) and a holy community dedicated to mutual love and forgiveness (chapter 18). To Jews who are uniting around their teachers in order to survive in the midst of a hostile world, he proposes the conquest of this world and the rejection of any hierarchy.[9] To those who are disturbed at the risks of such an option, he replies with the Beatitudes[10] and a repeated reminder of the Last Judgment (in particular chapter 25), which will restore their rights to all those who have been deprived of them in this world. Finally, to all those who fear that they are too weak to realize such an ambitious programme, the Risen Christ promises his permanent and omnipotent presence.[11]

As we noted in connection with the Letter of James, there is nothing to indicate that the Gospel of Matthew won any appreciable number of those at whom it was aimed over to the Christian faith. But no document allows us to conclude that it had no influence either. Be this as it may, the great majority of Jews were won over to the Pharisaic reform, which means that the Christian counter-offensive did not achieve its objectives. Towards the end of the first century, Christianity remained a small movement bringing together some tens of thousands of people, while Judaism, despite its misfortunes, still had millions of members, both within the Roman empire and beyond its Eastern frontier. What was to happen to the small Christian group, henceforth deprived of the protection of Jewish status in the Roman empire? Its survival did not seem assured, since it had not succeeded in winning over the Jewish majority to its ideas and it remained a very modest group within the pagan world. Its salvation came from its small Pauline minority.

11

A New Dawn for Paul's Heirs

On their return, crestfallen, to their home churches after being rebuffed in Jerusalem by James and his entourage and after the arrest and detention of Paul, the delegates of the communities founded by the apostle to the Gentiles certainly did not bring their brothers a message of encouragement. Reconciliation with the mother church was proving impossible; the majority of the Christian churches continued to regard the heirs of Paul as irresponsible people who were endangering all Christians, and from now on the great voice of the apostle was silent. It was even worse when Paul had perished and the Neronian persecution had shown how dangerous it was for Christians to distinguish themselves from Jews. When Judaism had been pierced to the heart in 70, and the Christians who had remained close to the synagogues set out to win disorientated Jews to the cause of Christ, the situation of Paul's heirs became even more embarrassing. They were the compromising brethren whom the others denied[1] in order to have the best chances of making the Jews listen.

So it is easy to understand how, around 70–80 CE, the churches which had arisen out of Paul's missionary activity showed the utmost discretion. The wave which drove the majority of their brethren towards the synagogues was too strong for them to resist. However, from the beginning of the 80s CE, the voice of the Pauline churches began to make itself heard again, at first timidly and then with growing boldness. Timidity still has the upper hand in the redaction of Luke-Acts, which we can put around 80–85 CE. Certainly this is a very ambitious work, which gives a long introduction to the gospel as Mark had presented it and above all a long continuation, extending the account of the gospel to the arrival of Paul in Rome. It is significant that a small group of churches had the will and the capacity to prompt such a remarkable work, which far surpassed all that Christianity had produced hitherto. However, there is something surprising about the apologetic tone of the whole work which merits investigation.

In fact a narrative ending in a kind of definitive affirmation of the

divine plan accomplished in the evangelization of the pagans is para-
doxically presented in Luke-Acts as a laborious demonstration of the
Jewish roots of this movement. The skilful combination of two traditions, one about the birth of John the Baptist and the other about the
birth of Jesus, allows the author to make his account begin in the
Temple of Jerusalem and in the most zealous Jewish pietist circles. The
report of Jesus' ministry which begins in Luke 4 certainly contains an
allusion to an activity directed towards the pagans,[2] but almost all the
scenes which the Gospel of Mark sets in pagan territory have been
suppressed in Luke. Certainly some of the miracles of Jesus are performed for pagans,[3] while one of his parables gives a Samaritan as an
example.[4] However, apart from a crossing of Samaria to get from
Galilee to Jerusalem,[5] Luke's Jesus never leaves Jewish Palestine. It is as
if his Jewishness had to be reaffirmed in the face of doubts expressed by
certain opponents. For the same reason two passages in the Gospel of
Mark in which Jesus questions the provisions of the Law[6] disappear in
the Gospel of Luke.

So one could suppose that Luke-Acts is the work of a Jewish
Christian, did not the book of Acts contradict this hypothesis. This
work is in fact devoted to a report of the transition of the gospel from
the Jews to the pagans, and its hero is the apostle Paul. So much is this
the case that the churches founded by Paul are the only setting which
could have given rise to Luke-Acts. But the apologetic that we find in
Luke also exists in Acts. The primitive church in Jerusalem is also
completely Jewish and addresses its preaching only to Jews, even on the
day of Pentecost.[7] The Hellenists, those bold spoilsports in the way in
which they challenge the Temple, address their preaching only to the
periphery of Judaism,[8] and not to pagans, until the day when in Acts 10
Peter opens up the way. Then they also address the Greeks, in Antioch.[9]
Moreover, the initiative in preaching to the pagans is not simply taken
by Peter; it is carefully prepared for and encouraged by God himself,[10]
who overcomes human reluctance. Before Paul becomes the apostle to
the pagans, he receives a divine call; he becomes an assistant to
Barnabas, always preaches in the synagogue before leaving it as a result
of the opposition that he encounters there, and turns to the pagans only
as a last resort.[11] It has often been said that this Paul was more conformist than the real Paul and that he remained far more Jewish than he
really was. There is no doubt about this, even if some critics have
de-Judaized the historical Paul too much. So it is very interesting to note
how much the author of Luke-Acts, a passionate admirer of the apostle

to the Gentiles, has tried to show that Paul never renounced his Judaism, that he only took the route opened up by Peter, and that he always followed the latter's example. Thus the scandal of Paul was trivialized and the Pauline churches did not show any originality compared with other churches, apart from their independence from the synagogues. In short, the Pauline Christians were no different from their brothers in the churches founded by Peter, Barnabas and the other missionaries, whether in origin, doctrine or behaviour. There was no justification whatsoever for their separation. This very skilful and very impressive plea made by literary means was the first and still timid attempt by the Pauline churches grouped around the Aegean Sea to resume their place in the communion of Christian churches, at a time when these remained very Jewish and were trying to win brothers from among the members of the synagogues.[12]

This first effort, still bearing the stamp of a certain feeling of inferiority, was followed by another, which was already more enterprising. Around 85–90 the Pauline churches thought that they could give advice and practical examples to the other Christian communities which would help these to organize themselves when the time of their expulsion from the synagogues was looming, as the Pharisaic reform progressed. That is the origin of the so-called 'Pastoral'[13] Epistles attributed to Paul. They are so different from the other letters in style and thought that we have to see them as the work of disciples of the apostle. They could have reused some of Paul's authentic notes, but above all they spoke in his name. The pastoral advice that they put under the patronage of a Paul who has at last achieved respectability is often quite down-to-earth. Paul is thought to be communicating the content of his experience, with his own authority, to the leaders of communities whose organization is still tentative. The literary fiction which makes two close colleagues of the apostle to the Gentiles, Timothy[14] and Titus,[15] the recipients of Paul's advice and warnings barely disguises the real beneficiaries of this help, namely the leaders of communities which are still somewhat experimental. These could be churches which had been founded recently. It is just as likely that the communities envisaged already had a relatively long history but had somewhat belatedly found themselves obliged to organize independently when, with the progress of the Pharisaic reform of the synagogues, the very convenient framework provided by the latter had disappeared. So these churches needed ministries corresponding to all the needs of communal life: *episcopoi*,[16] elders,[17] deacons,[18] widows responsible for providing help.[19] The definition of these various functions is never made very precise, but it is clear that they correspond to the needs of teaching, discipline and material and pastoral help felt by the independent communities. The ministry entrusted to Timothy and Titus is not specified, but to all appearances it is defined as an extension of that of the apostle: evangelization, teaching, the organization of ministries, and the supervision of their activities in several communities. A discipline is also sketched out which is as applicable to ministers as it is to the faithful.[20] Moreover the task of organizing the church also has a doctrinal dimension. There is a need to do away with Judaizing doctrines, associated with the Law,[21] legends and Jewish fables,[22] and the prohibition of certain foods.[23] There is also a need to avoid aberrant doctrines, like the assertion that the resurrection has already taken place,[24] and to keep firmly outside anyone who propagates them.[25] Faithfulness to traditional doctrine is recommended, but its content is not specified.[26] In short, what counts in the life of the community is good order and the practice of bourgeois virtues, which support piety towards the Risen Christ. None of this is incompatible with the message of Paul, but it is only a very pale copy of it.[27]

Thus when the Pauline churches dared to abandon their defensive attitude and to suggest to other Christians a model of church organization which claimed the authority of Paul, they were not bold enough to allow the historical Paul to speak and to present his gospel in all its radical nature. However, the Letter to the Ephesians, also composed around 85–90, tries to go further and to present a much more basic ecclesiology, taking further Paul's ideas on the body of Christ.

The Letter to the Ephesians, which from the start presents itself as the work of Paul, differs greatly from the other letters of the apostle, with the exception of the Letter to the Colossians, to which it displays a number of parallels. These also pose the problem of the literary relationship between the two texts. Since some basic differences make it difficult to attribute the two writings to the same author, we are led to suppose that the Letter to the Ephesians, a kind of encyclical whose intended recipients are somewhat uncertain,[28] is the work of a disciple of Paul who used the Letter to the Colossians as a model. So here we shall see a work contemporary with the Pastoral Epistles, also intended to meet the needs of Christians who have been progressively eliminated from the synagogues by offering them under the name of Paul elements of doctrine which justify the formation of independent churches. Unlike the Pastoral Epistles, there is no practical advice here, but basic justifications. A first part (chapters 1 to 3) develops the idea that the formation of a church which unites Jews and pagans is the outcome of the divine work of which Paul has been the agent. A second part (chapters 4–6) exhorts believers to behave in keeping with their vocation as members of the body of Christ. Contrary to the Pastoral Epistles, the question of ministries is touched on only in passing,[29] and all the emphasis is put on the morality which members of the community must observe. All this is very close to Paul's thought, but differs from it in the very strong emphasis put on the universal church, whereas the apostle to the Gentiles emphasized the life of the local community.[30]

Thus Paul's heirs are not content with suggesting models for the organization of the local churches which are obliged to form outside the synagogues. They also state the principles which must underlie the existence of the church and Christian morality, in the hope that their brothers from the non-Pauline communities will find the basis for their own independent existence there.

Paul's heirs had one last step to take in order to make their full contribution to the life of Christianity at the end of the first century CE: to make the authentic texts of Paul available to all those who had not known them. They did not dare to do this until around 95 CE, since the schismatic and heretic to whom they owed everything remained an object of scandal in most churches, while some of his writings were still offensive because they were so violent. One has only to think of the Letter to the Galatians! As the reform of the synagogues progressed and the gulf between Judaism and Christianity grew deeper, these reservations lost much of their meaning. Paul had been given a voice with the public launching of the Pastoral Epistles and the Letter to the Ephesians. Why not let him speak for himself from now on?

As we have seen, during the ten or so years during which he had been an independent missionary Paul had resorted to writing in order to encourage, teach, reprimand or advise the churches which he had founded when he was separated from them by tasks that he had elsewhere. At that time his letters were one of his means of action, along with sending one or other of his fellow workers or even paying a personal visit. We do not know how many letters he wrote. Certainly some were only short notes, a large number of which have not survived. Others, which are mentioned in the New Testament letters, have also disappeared or were subsequently integrated into one or other of the letters which found a place in the canon.[31] Yet others appear in the canonical collection, but we cannot be sure that they have not had cuts made, been added to, or even fused with another correspondence. These uncertainties are easy to explain. When a local church had received a letter from Paul it would read it in the assembly at public worship, perhaps several times in succession. Then, as the situation developed, it would put this precious document in its archives, which in most cases were doubtless not very well kept. The difficulties experienced by many communities, the damage caused by water, fire, rats and so on, destroyed or damaged many of these texts, which in any case had been written in haste on poor-quality papyrus.

The church leader who, after several earlier efforts, decided shortly before 95 to bring together the letters of Paul, faced a difficult task. He had not only to collect the documents existing in the archives of at least half a dozen churches but also to fill the gaps in the manuscripts, combine incomplete fragments, put end to end separate texts apparently addressed to the same recipients, and so on. In some cases, as for example with the Letter to the Romans, he doubtless had two or more manuscripts which had to be compared and perhaps combined. There can be no question here of entering the maze of hypotheses constructed to decipher these interventions. What matters for us is the result of this great operation.

The collection of Paul's letters which appeared around 95 consisted of thirteen letters, four of which (the Pastorals and Ephesians) were certainly by disciples of the apostle writing a generation after his death. This collection, the order of which varied, forms rather less than a quarter of the New Testament. It is a bit shorter than Luke-Acts, which is the most important literary block in the New Testament. The length of the letters that make it up varies from one to sixteen chapters, but all present themselves as letters from the apostle Paul, often accompanied by one or more fellow-workers. Four out of the thirteen letters are addressed to one individual, while the others are addressed to the Christians of a particular city or, in the case of Galatia, of a province. Although such a collection of letters was not very long, it corresponded to a literary genre known in Greco-Roman culture, So it could be copied and circulated, not only among the church public, but also in educated circles of the Roman empire, where curiosity about Christianity was beginning to be aroused.[32]

That having been said, the main readers of such a collection could only have been Christians, given the content of the letters in question. We can easily imagine the shock that reading these letters must have caused among people used to a more ingratiating style and less vigorous thought than that of Paul. The remark made around 125 CE by the author of the second letter of Peter gives some idea of the reactions aroused by contact with the Pauline corpus:

> So also our beloved brother Paul wrote to you according to the wisdom given him, speaking of this as he does in all his letters. There are some things in them which are hard to understand, which the ignorant and unstable twist to their own destruction, as they do the other scriptures.[33]

One could hardly express better the mixture of respect, perplexity and mistrust that the majority of Christians must have felt at the dissemination of this collection. Thanks to the obstinacy of his heirs, the apostle to the Gentiles had emerged from the purgatory in which the Christian majority had imprisoned him since the middle of the first century. But he remained controversial and his letters lent themselves to many regrettable exploitations. That doubtless explains why the Christian authors of the second century refer to Paul very little and rarely use his vocabulary. Only Marcion (around 85–160) took him really seriously. He made the Pauline letters, after eliminating the Pastoral Epistles, an essential part of his holy scripture, intended to replace the Old Testament. It is symptomatic that it should have been this schismatic, and a heretic to boot, who should have dared to give Paul his true place. The great church continued to show reservations towards the apostle to the Gentiles, as is also shown by the way in which for a long time the Acts of the Apostles, separated from the Gospel of Luke from the beginning of the second century onwards, was relegated to the category of writings without authority. Clearly the only reason for this separation, which lasted almost a century, was the privileged place which Paul enjoys in this work.

Thus within barely twenty years Paul's heirs, at first mute until around 80 CE because of the demise of their master, had rediscovered the courage to affirm themselves and communicate to their brethren who had remained close to the synagogues all the riches of the tradition preserved by their small group of churches. They did so with increasing audacity and a remarkable literary talent, but did not succeed in convincing the Christian majority to go over unreservedly to Paulinism at a time when its links with Judaism were being completely broken. This semi-setback, which was one of the causes of the violent controversies which marked Christian history in the second century, was gradually remedied in successive centuries, until the day when Augustine gave Paul and his thought the place of honour which truly befits this great theologian.

12

Towards an Adult Christianity

Around 100 CE, the links between the Christian churches and the synagogues had been broken almost everywhere. Granted, as late as 95, the repression launched by the emperor Domitian against some people in his entourage, including a certain Flavius Clemens, who were accused of atheism and Jewish customs, did not make a clear distinction between converts to Judaism and adherents to Christianity.[1] But in 107–108, Ignatius, Bishop of Antioch, endured martyrdom in Rome as a Christian, and around 112 the persecutions against the Christians of Bithynia were directed against the disciples of Christ, who were no longer confused with the Jews.[2] In the same period Christians proved to be completely different from Jews.

Outside these episodes of persecution we know almost nothing about the events which stamped Christian history at the very end of the first century and the beginning of the second.[3] As in the preceding period, we are reduced to analysing the literary production of this period in order to understand the situation and the mentality of Christians. Fortunately this literature is quite extensive and gives us some fairly precise indications. A first group of texts, very different and of greatly varying importance, is formed by documents relating to the life of the churches, which also include moral exhortations. One very distinctive text, the Letter to the Hebrews, devoted to a powerful christological reflection, must be examined separately. Finally, the Johannine writings, less the Second and Third Letters of John, form a third group, characterized by an original and vigorous theological thought. They seem to be the expression of a school, but also the blossoming of a theology which has been emancipated from Judaism. This classification of Christian writings from the very end of the first century does not follow any geographical criterion nor does it base the division on well-defined tendencies. It seeks to be merely functional and empirical.

The first writing of the first group is the Didache (= teaching), a short text which presents itself as the work of the twelve apostles and certainly dates from shortly before the end of the first century. All scholars accept that it originated in Syria. The work begins with moral teaching on the theme of the two ways, those of good and evil.[4] This recalls the content of the Qumran Community Rule, but there is abundant reference to sayings of Jesus reported by the Synoptic Gospels. A second part[5] is a liturgical instruction about baptism, fasting, prayer and the eucharist. The third is a list of disciplinary rules[6] relating above all to the ministers of the church and marked by clear reservations about itinerant apostles and prophets. It does not dare to reject them completely, but prefers the bishops and deacons chosen by members of the community. The last chapter (16), which concludes the work, is devoted above all to evoking the return of the Lord. This text with its modest dimensions, which does not touch on any doctrinal subject, was doubtless aimed at village churches which wanted to do the right thing, but were hardly troubled by the great theological problems. Despite the numerous allusions to scripture in the first part, which uses a scheme of moral instruction deriving from Judaism, it is striking to note that Judaism is completely absent from the author's horizon. Here we find Christian communities which no longer have any dealings with the synagogues.[7]

The Second and Third Letters of John, which present themselves as notes written by 'the Elder',[8] closely resemble the First Letter of John in style and thought. We shall be discussing this last letter in due course. However, they do not have its breadth or its ambition. Their place of composition can be put in the Roman province of Asia, but their dating is very uncertain, though there is every possibility that it is before the end of the first century. In very different language, these two notes deal with the same subject as chapters 11 to 15 of the Didache: relations between the local communities and the itinerant ministries. The first of them warns a local church against visitors with a more or less heretical christology;[9] the second is reacting against the refusal of the leader of a community, a certain Diotrephes, to receive emissaries from the Elder.[10] Although relations with Judaism are not mentioned anywhere in these two writings, in them we discover self-sufficient communities which the author, who has a regional authority, is trying to keep under his control.[11]

The Letter of Clement of Rome to the Corinthians is generally dated to around 95. It is a much more important document than those previously mentioned. Its author, who does not identify himself, speaks in the name of the church of Rome. Various indications converge to allow us to identify him with Clement, one of the bishops of Rome around

90–100. This is a real letter, intended for the church of Corinth, and marked with a certain solemnity, as befits official correspondence. After long preliminaries in a somewhat flowery style and in keeping with the rules of epistolary politeness, the author finally comes to the point, from chapter 45 on. Although he continues to speak in a lofty tone, he criticizes the divisions which have come about among the Corinthians and calls upon them to restore their functions to the bishops and elders whom they had deposed. He then launches into a long prayer[12] and ends with a last appeal to them to restore the situation which existed before the crisis.[13] Despite the difference in style, we find here the spirit of the texts which have already been mentioned: the Christian church has to have its own organization and lead a totally independent life, even if it makes abundant use of the Jewish scriptures. It will also be noted that the church of Corinth, once founded by Paul, was quite used to this idea. But it has to be exhorted to more stability and faithfulness to its own institutions. The fact that the church of Rome is launching this appeal shows the progress made towards a more permanent organization by the Christians of the capital who, thirty or forty years earlier, had not yet succeeded in uniting to form a church. In this case, the breaking of the links with the synagogue has resulted in a reinforcement of church structure.[14]

The letters of Ignatius of Antioch are the work of a bishop of Antioch in Syria who was condemned to death by the Romans. They were written to several of the churches of the province of Asia and to that of the imperial capital, doubtless around 107–108, while Ignatius was being transported to Rome, where he was to be executed. The person who reveals himself here with a good deal of spontaneity is attractive and impressive in his determination not to shrink from suffering and death, in imitation of Jesus and in order to rediscover him in the world beyond.[15] Here and there in his letters Ignatius produces very bold christological formulae which already prefigure classical doctrine.[16] He vigorously denounces the heretics who deny the reality of the incarnation and the death of Christ.[17] He firmly distinguishes himself from Judaism and its practices.[18] He is the first author to use the term 'Christianity', which he opposes to Judaism. The break between the two religions is now complete. Furthermore, Ignatius attaches great importance to the bishop, who for him is the sole leader of the local church and the local representative of God.[20] He teaches us that from the beginning of the second century the churches of the province of Asia had opted for a monarchical episcopate, while at the same time many other communities including those of Rome and Corinth were still combining bishops and elders. Alongside this sole bishop, Ignatius attaches much importance to the college of elders,[21] which he compares to that of the apostles, and to the deacons,[22] whom he says must be venerated as though they were Jesus Christ. In short, Ignatius bears witness to the existence of churches which had become completely alien to Judaism and which were quite firmly organized around their bishop and their other ministers.[23]

Some years later, the letter of Polycarp, bishop of Smyrna, to the Philippians, which is all that we now have of a larger correspondence, mentions the same topics as the letters of Ignatius. These are: traditional theology and christology,[24] indications of the twofold ministry of elders and deacons,[25] moral exhortations for the whole of the community[26] and for certain groups like women, widows, young people and virgins.[27] The main difference is that Polycarp, doubtless addressing a church in which elders and bishops were not combined, does not mention the ministry of the bishop. In short, this author attests that the local churches were organized quite independently and in different ways, and that they were preoccupied above all with their internal existence. Relations with the civil authorities are reduced to intercession on their behalf,[28] and the perspective of sufferings arising out of their action is only alluded to very indirectly.[29] Finally, it will also be noted that Polycarp avers that he has little knowledge of the ancient scriptures,[30] which he cites rarely,[31] while he is fond of referring to the Gospels of Matthew and Luke, to the Acts of the Apostles and above all to the letters of Paul, the Letter to the Hebrews, the First Letter of Peter and the First Letter of John. In his eyes these are not yet holy scripture, but for him they have great authority, as is also the case with the letters of Ignatius of Antioch.[32]

The christological treatise which has come to be called the Letter to the Hebrews is quite different from these short occasional works. This text is anonymous and has none of the characteristics of a letter except in the last four verses,[33] which were perhaps added later. These contain some news, some salutations and a benediction which resembles those that we find in the correspondence of the time. The date of composition is prior to 95 CE, since the letter of Clement of Rome to the Corinthians cites the document; however, despite the arguments advanced by some critics, it is not much before this, since the separation between Judaism and Christianity would seem to be complete in Hebrews, even if the author makes abundant use of the Old Testament. There is no way of identifying precisely those to whom it is addressed, the mysterious 'Hebrews', who are not mentioned anywhere in the text. Since the document became part of the collection of Paul's letters at a very early stage, it can be accepted that the epistolary conclusion and the title were added to the text when it was included in the Pauline corpus, to present it in a form somewhat comparable to that of the previous letters. The term 'Hebrews' could then have been suggested by the content of the work, with the cult as its theme.

This somewhat mysterious document is also quite original. Written in a rather elegant Greek, it is at the same time the New Testament book which is most fond of quoting and commenting on the Old Testament. Its interpretation of the ancient texts has analogies with the hermeneutics of Qumran, and also with that of Philo of Alexandria. However, it does not derive from either. The author has a thesis to demonstrate and makes use of scripture to do so. He succeeds in this very easily and with much talent. Although the end of the writing contains moral exhortations which belong in a church context, with rulers to be respected,[34] assemblies to be attended[35] and oppositions to be endured,[36] the greater part of the work is devoted to original christological reflection, which is clearly different from the christology of the Synoptic tradition, Paul and the Johannine school, while basing itself constantly on Holy Scripture. One has the feeling that the author, freed from any dependence on Judaism, feels authorized to re-read the biblical writings in his own way, to find in them his doctrine of Christ. For him, the prescriptions of the Law about sacrifices or in the area of food[37] are no more than prefigurations of the mission of Christ and allegories of the Christian life. He does not even need to denounce the hold they have on some brethren, as Paul had had to do when Christians still remained within Judaism. The separation between Christianity and Judaism has been made, so thoroughly that the literal interpretation of the commandments has become unthinkable.

It is thanks to this emancipation from the literal meaning of the law that the author can develop his thesis of Christ as priest and high priest. Since Jesus had not had the slightest priestly character, by his origin, his activity, or his suffering and death, the Letter to the Hebrews makes the titles of priest and high priest the designation of Christ *par excellence*. By his suffering and his glorification, by his constant intercession with God on behalf of human beings, Christ is the 'great high priest',[38] who attains this status 'after the order of Melchizedek',[39] i.e. with more legitimacy than the priests who are descended from Aaron. He has offered his own life as a unique offering,[40] which makes the sacrifices prescribed by the law obsolete. From now on he has opened up access to God for human beings.[41] The question whether believers belong to the chosen people, over which there was still such a debate thirty or forty years earlier, does not arise at all. We may note that terms like 'circumcision' and 'uncircumcision', which are so frequent in Paul, have completely disappeared from the Letter to the Hebrews. Nothing shows better the distance that has been established between Judaism and Christianity at the end of the first century.[42]

The three writings which tradition has brought together around the person of John form the third complex which illustrates the independence and maturity of Christianity around the end of the first century. We shall not return to the Second and Third Letters of John, brief occasional works which have already been mentioned, even if there is quite a close relationship between these two texts and the First Letter of John. The three texts which we shall be examining here are very different from one another: an anonymous Gospel – the fourth in the New Testament; a 'letter' which has no other link with the epistolary genre than the repeated use by the anonymous author of the expression 'my little children'; and an apocalypse which offers a gripping picture of the end of the present world, attributing this description to someone called John. A certain affinity of style and vocabulary, the attribution of the Gospel and the Letter by tradition to John, and a probable geographical and chronological proximity allow us to group these three texts together, though they should not be mixed up; each should be examined separately.

The Apocalypse of John undoubtedly belongs to the apocalyptic genre, well known in intertestamental Jewish literature. It has the same mysterious language, a tendency to divide history into chronological periods, a visionary and dramatic character, and a taste for descriptions of heavenly scenes. However, unlike almost all apocalypses, it is not put under the patronage of a famous figure of the past and is rooted in a Roman province, that of Asia, which in no way is a holy place. The most probable dating of the final redaction puts the work around the end of the reign of Domitian, i.e. about 95 CE. It is complex, and some of the elements which go to make it up were doubtless composed earlier. However, what interests us here is its final state.

The Apocalypse of John was composed in a time of crisis and threat.

The author, an exile on the island of Patmos 'for the word of God and the testimony of Jesus',[43] in a period of great trial for the churches of the province of Asia, which were threatened by the development of emperor worship during the reign of Domitian, has received a heavenly vision there. He addresses an account of it to seven churches in this province, situated in Ephesus, Smyrna, Pergamum, Thyatira, Sardes, Philadelphia and Laodicea. He begins by writing a letter to each of these communities, dictated by the risen Christ.[44] These missives refer to the concrete situation of the seven churches: many of them have experienced persecution or are about to undergo it (Smyrna, Pergamum, Philadelphia); two of them are in conflict with the local synagogue (Smyrna, Philadelphia), which the author politely calls a 'synagogue of Satan'; three of the communities (Ephesus, Sardes and Laodicea) have lost their first fervour in various ways; several of them are confronted with heretical movements which they are getting rid of more or less well. The hallmark of all these heretical movements is that they allow Christians to take part in idolatrous cults (Ephesus, Pergamum, Thyatira). In short, these are communities independent from Judaism; some of their members at least are tempted to become integrated into the surrounding society and its religion. The Risen Christ exhorts them in different ways, depending on their situation: he announces his visit to all and makes magnificent promises to the 'conquerors'.

From the beginning of chapter 4 the seer reports his vision, with an extraordinary wealth of images and symbols very largely drawn from the Old Testament and intertestamental literature. It has also been suggested that Christian worship, from now on organized outside the synagogues and the liturgy of synagogue meetings, provided much of the material for the descriptions of heavenly worship given by the author. Many of the pictures and accounts in this text are deliberately mysterious and difficult to decipher; this is a law of the apocalyptic genre. Thus the identification of the two witnesses of chapter 11 and of the 'great city' (11.8) where they underwent martyrdom is almost impossible. Similarly, the drama of the woman and the dragon in chapter 12 is extremely difficult to interpret. By contrast, it is clear how hostile the author is towards Rome,[45] the total destruction of which is the prelude to the triumph of the Lamb (chapter 19). The thousand-year reign of the Messiah, surrounded by risen martyrs, is destined to take the place of the hated Roman empire. However, the eschatological perspective goes much further, towards a new Jerusalem which has come down from heaven to set itself at the heart of the new earth. This miraculous city in which God dwells with his own no longer has any need for a temple (chapters 21–22), since the communion between the redeemed community and its God is total. We may guess that this depiction of the eschatological fulfilment is aimed at making the gulf between Christians and Jews impossible to cross, since the latter retained the hope of a rebuilding of the Jerusalem temple at the end of time.[46]

The Gospel of John, and the First Letter which goes under the name of John in the tradition, have only distant relations with the colourful pictures of the Apocalypse, even if we accept that there is a relationship between these three writings. Both the Letter and the Gospel are characterized by a limited vocabulary, clumsy syntax and a very repetitive style which suggest an author whose mother tongue was not Greek. We may guess at a complex prehistory for these two writings; this is not the place to explore it, but it certainly explains the presence of numerous elements akin to the sectarian Judaism of Palestine. The final redaction of the two works could have taken place in the region of Ephesus, though we have no proof of this. Critics are divided over the order in which the Gospel and the Letter were composed in their definitive form. However, the balance of opinion tends to favour the priority of the Letter, which could be dated around 90, while the Gospel would go back to the years 100–110. The author of the First Letter of John is not named anywhere in the work. He often speaks in the first person plural, as the spokesman of a group of witnesses to the earthly ministry of Jesus Christ,[47] but more often still in the first person singular,[48] addressing brothers whom he cherishes.[49] These are also his spiritual children[50] and he is sufficiently close to them to be able to use 'we' often in speaking of them.[51] In short, he is speaking to them as a spiritual father who shares in the life of the community, even when he addresses them as 'you' or when he mentions Christian behaviour in the third person singular, which he also does.

There is a very strong emphasis on the mutual love which binds the brethren together.[52] We are faced with a tightly knit community for which the outer world is repulsive.[53] The community is based on the forgiveness of sins procured by Jesus Christ, whose sacrifice purifies it.[54] From him it receives light,[55] the commandment to love,[56] the knowledge of God,[57] the Holy Spirit[58] and eternal life,[59] while the world remains in darkness, practices hatred of neighbour, does not know God, is moved by a spirit of evil and is rushing towards death. The opposition between the holy community and the world imprisoned in sin is as radical as it is at Qumran, where the same pairs of terms recur. So we cannot exclude an Essene influence on the Johannine community from which this letter has come. However, this influence is certainly an old one. At the time of the definitive redaction of the text, what is most striking is the absence of any reference to the life of the synagogue and the rarity of allusions to the Jewish scriptures. The church from which this letter comes is very detached from Judaism. On the other hand, it is struggling with heretical tendencies which it feels to be a danger: they deny the sinful state of humanity[60] and the messiahship of Jesus[61] and reject the commandment to love.[62] Gnostic tendencies have been envisaged in this connection. At all events, what we seem to have here is an individualism led to speculate about God and opposed to the consolidation of organized Christian communities. The Gnostic groups and their elitist intellectualism are not very far away, while like Paul, our author is set on the formation of communities independent of the synagogues but with as firm a structure as they have.[63]

The Fourth Gospel may be regarded as the most perfect expression of a Christianity which has reached maturity. Certainly, as I have already remarked, this is a complex writing, with a complex prehistory going back to the Palestinian Christianity of the 40s and 50s CE. A group of disciples, doubtless gathered around the apostle John, son of Zebedee, seems to have formed on the periphery of the Jerusalem church. It seems to have drawn to a far greater degree than the majority of that church on many ideas in the vast reservoir of sectarian Judaism, particularly among the Essenes, in order to reflect on the person and work of Jesus Christ. This group would have fled Palestine during the Jewish War of 66–70, and at least some of its members will have taken refuge in the province of Asia, more specifically at Ephesus, where second-century tradition puts the residence of the apostle John. Since they remained peripheral to the church of Ephesus which Paul founded around a dozen years later, the members of this group could have maintained links with the synagogue of Ephesus, which the apostle to the Gentile had left three months after his arrival in the city (Acts 19.9). Their collective activity within the framework of the synagogue had not met with any organizational problems and had retained a meditative and doubtless liturgical character.

A quarter of a century after they had settled in Ephesus, the Pharisaic reform was implemented by the synagogue leaders, who excluded from their assembly the marginal groups which hitherto had been easily tolerated, but which from now on had become an annoyance. Among those who were excluded was the small 'Johannine' community; we know that some years later it still had a bitter memory of this expulsion,[64] which doubtless had had some brutal features. It could be that another group of marginal Jews suffered the same fate: that of the disciples of John the Baptist, whose presence in this region dated to before Paul's arrival.[65] That would explain the presence in the first chapters of the Fourth Gospel of a significant number of passages relating to John the Baptist and his disciples, several of which have a polemical tone. This requires an explanation.[66] The most probable reason for this surprising confrontation three-quarters of a century after the baptism of Jesus by John the Baptist is that the two groups driven from the synagogue suddenly found themselves rivals in the eyes of the non-Jewish circles to whom they had been sent. We shall return later to this situation, which was a new one for the two communities.

Exclusion from the synagogue of Ephesus, rivalry with the disciples of John the Baptist and a now inevitable rapprochement with the communities which had arisen out of Paul's activity, were all reasons for the composition of the Fourth Gospel, which must be put around 100–110 of our era. The bearers of a tradition of their own which went back more than half a century, and thrown into a situation which made it necessary for them to engage in deep theological reflection on their faith and their community organization, the disciples of John, son of Zebedee, whose extreme longevity is reported by legend and who had left a permanent mark on his followers, sought to express their christology and all their sensitivity in an important literary work. Instead of adopting the genre of the theological treatise, like the Letter to the Hebrews, or that of the letter, like Paul's Letter to the Romans, they opted for the literary genre of the Gospel. Whatever scholars may have said, they certainly knew the Gospels of Mark and Luke. Without imitating these writings too slavishly, at all events they derived from them the idea of a presentation of the person of Jesus which was at the same time both biographical and theological. The genre had a good deal of success among the faithful and among the missionaries' audiences. It was capable of reaching a much wider audience than a theological treatise or a letter would have done, because of its attractive mixture of narratives and discourses. Thus was born the masterpiece that we call the Fourth Gospel; to judge from several converging indications, it spread rapidly in the Christian churches, but also in marginal areas, like the first Gnostic circles.

This work, rather longer than the Gospel of Mark and rather

shorter than those of Matthew and Luke, is constructed on the same model as its three predecessors: an account of the public ministry of Jesus, preceded by a prologue and followed by an account of the passion and some appearances of the risen Christ. However, there are numerous differences between it and the Synoptic Gospels, even if it has many narratives in common with them, beginning with the passion narrative. This is not the place to list them; it is enough to note just a few. Instead of grouping the scenes which take place in Jerusalem just before the account of the passion, the Fourth Gospel divides them into several groups;[67] the result of this is to give them more importance, all the more so since there are also the farewell discourses in chapters 13 to 17. The miracle stories are at the same time fewer and far more spectacular than those in the Synoptics; the teachings of Jesus do not have much in common with the aphorisms and parables of the Synoptic Gospels, but form long discourses, the internal organization of which is often obscure. Despite these differences, it seems that the Fourth Gospel, like its predecessors, is based on a tradition some of the elements of which are certainly of Palestinian origin. However, this is not identical with the Synoptic tradition and bears the stamp of a process of original transmission within a group devoted to christological meditation.

One of the most striking features of the Fourth Gospel is the frequent use of the term 'the Jews' to denote the interlocutors and adversaries of Jesus (it occurs 71 times, as opposed to 5 or 6 in each of the other Gospels). All the signs are that in the eyes of the author this is a group to which Christians do not belong, because they have been expelled from it. Here is the language of those who consider themselves to be outside Judaism. The use of the word 'Pharisees', which is no more frequent than in the Synoptics, is close to that in the Gospel of Matthew. Like that Gospel, the Gospel of John reflects the reorganization of the synagogues undertaken by the reformers of the school of Jamnia and the conviction that this group was the main opponent of Christianity.[68] On this point, too, we can see that despite the Jewish roots of his thought, the author of the Fourth Gospel stands outside the Judaism of his time, which he no longer hopes to be able to win over to Christ, in contrast to the evangelist Matthew. It will also be noted that his Jesus, utterly Jewish though he was, does not have a Jewish genealogy like those in Matthew and Luke because he is the divine word incarnate (1.14). His ministry begins with a transfiguration of the Jewish practices of purity[69] and the desacralization of the Jerusalem Temple,[70] i.e. with gestures preparing for a supersession of Judaism.

Despite these indications of the de-Judaization of Christianity, the Fourth Gospel continues to be dominated by the difficult question of the meaning of the separation between Judaism and Christianity. The author tries to avoid an interpretation of the break as a simple accident. Like the evangelist Matthew, he traces the confrontation back to the time of Jesus, and this allows him to see it as the realization of a divine plan bound up with the mission of Christ. But instead of putting the responsibility for it on the 'scribes and Pharisees, hypocrites',[71] he introduces an aggressive Jesus who attacks all 'the Jews',[72] even when these believe in him. True faith in this heavenly being is impossible for human beings, even though they may be Jews, if they are reduced to their own strength. It becomes possible only after the raising up of Christ to the Father, through the gift of the Holy Spirit to the disciples.[73]

So the divine nature of Jesus is an essential factor, which largely explains why it is impossible for the Jews to go over to the one who had come among them. A human messiah would quite naturally have secured the adherence of a large number of his compatriots. The Johannine Jesus himself aroused individual and collective enthusiasms among the Jews by his actions and his words. But he refused to trust in these enthusiasms and did what he needed to do to discourage those who were moved by them, since their faith was fatally based on misunderstandings about his person.[74] The only followers who were acceptable during Jesus' ministry were some who benefitted from his miracles,[75] some on the periphery of Judaism,[76] and a certain number of disciples who went directly or indirectly through the hands of John the Baptist,[77] the prophet charged by God to bear witness to the divinity of Jesus.[78] These disciples prepared by the Baptist are presented as given by God the Father to Jesus and protected by him.[79] It is through them that the world will be evangelized.

Here we rediscover the polemic directed against the disciples of John the Baptist, apparently effective rivals of the Christian missionaries, with a message which identified their master with the Messiah and reduced Jesus to the status of a more or less unfaithful pupil. Some passages in the Fourth Gospel suggest the existence of quite lively competition between the two groups which had recently been excluded from the synagogue and had been obliged to turn to sympathizers of Judaism put off by the Pharisaic reform or to the pagans. Although the remark in 4.1–2 only serves to introduce a phrase relating to a journey of Jesus, it is very revealing in this connection, all the more so since it emphasizes the role of the disciples. The little story in 3.22–26 is even more significant, since it evokes the vexation felt by the disciples of the Baptist at the tremendous success of Jesus' preaching. And while the little parable in John 4.35–38 attributes the cultivation of Samaria to the disciples of the Baptist, it attributes the harvest on the same soil to Jesus' disciples. This suggests that the outcome could have been different. The author of the Fourth Gospel has chosen the most effective weapon for reducing the spokesmen of Baptist circles to silence: he has given John the Baptist only the role of bearing witness to the superiority of Jesus. The Synoptic evangelists had already taken this line, which is particularly visible in Mark. However, our author goes much further. He in no way denigrates the Baptist, whose calling the Prologue mentions in strong terms.[80] However, he denies him the title Baptist and only makes a vague allusion to his activity as a preacher and a baptizer.[81] He eliminates the account of the baptism of Jesus by John the Baptist, replacing it with vague allusions.[82] All this suggests that the divine forgiveness is procured by the work of Jesus Christ and not by the baptism of John,[83] since the sole aim of the latter is to allow the revelation of Jesus.[84] Moreover the author of the Fourth Gospel puts vigorous denials of his own messiahship on the lips of John the Baptist.[85] On the other hand, the witness given by the precursor to Jesus is presented emphatically,[86] and is full of radical formulae emphasizing his divine origin and his redemptive mission. In short, here John the Baptist contradicts everything that his supporters say of him and lends his support to the one whom they wanted to reduce to their purely human level.

Thus rid of awkward rivals, the disciples of Jesus, recruited at the beginning of the ministry of their Master,[87] and purged by the departure of some who had been discouraged by the discourse on the bread of life[88] and of the traitor Judas,[89] benefit from the symbolic gesture of the foot-washing[90] and the teaching which Jesus gives them before his passion.[91] They receive the promise of the Holy Spirit, which will give them the supernatural power to make their hearers understand everything, remaining in full communion with the risen Christ and with God the Father. Despite all persecutions and all opposition, they will be able to 'overcome the world'[92] and to win many people over to the faith.[93] The gift of the Holy Spirit is made to them on the first appearance of the Risen Christ,[94] at the same time as they are sent into the world with a supernatural authority to forgive sins.[95] This is the prefiguration of a church – although the word does not feature in the vocabulary of the Fourth Gospel – which is solidly attached to the heritage of the first disciples of Jesus. So the communities excluded from the synagogues are not more or less disorientated groups, but direct heirs of the primitive preaching, and their legitimacy goes back to the most distant origins. Nothing is said about their organization and their everyday life, but it is clear that they have ministers who are successors of the apostles. They celebrate the eucharist[96] and baptism,[97] and their community life is based on the commandment to love one another.[98] This must lead to unity, within the communities and between them.[99] The author of the Fourth Gospel is aware of the divisions which exist between the Christian groups of his time and has an 'ecumenical' aspiration, the con- crete realization of which is required by God through Christ in his priestly prayer in chapter 17.[100]

Thus around the year 100 CE, Christians stopped engaging in polemic against the synagogue and presenting themselves as the most authentic Jews. From now on they knew that they were alone in the vast world and tried to think out this new situation without giving up their roots in the Jewish scriptures and the brief earthly ministry of Jesus. Their christology and their ecclesiology took on definitive form. Adulthood, with its new set of problems, was approaching for Christianity.

13

Consolidation and Hellenization

The break between Judaism and Christianity which was completed in the last years of the first century was irrevocable. The Christians of pagan origin, who were ever more numerous in the churches, did not feel the slightest nostalgia for a recent past in which their communities lived in close dependence on the synagogue. The Jews, who had been given a clear awareness of their identity by their Pharisaic rabbis, from now on took far less interest in the pagan world which surrounded them. The disappearance of the apologetic and missionary literature which had proliferated in the previous period is the best indication of this. Moreover, dramatic events were to deepen the gulf between Jews and Christians. Between 115 and 117 Jews rebelled against Roman domination on Cyprus, in Egypt and Cyrenaica, and in Mesopotamia, which had just been conquered by Rome from the Parthian empire. Contrary to what had probably happened in 66–70, the Christians did not associate themselves with this revolt in any way. That certainly helped to convince the authorities to draw a clear distinction between them and the Jews. So it was that in 124–125 the emperor Hadrian addressed a rescript to Caius Minucius Fundanus, proconsul of Asia, ordering him not to allow Christians to be accused without proof (Justin Martyr quotes this text at the end of his First Apology, around 135). We know that Hadrian was personally hostile to Judaism and that he repressed with great brutality the new Jewish revolt which took place in 132–135 under the leadership of a certain Bar Kochba, mainly in Palestine. The complete destruction of Jerusalem, which was turned into Aelia Capitolina and prohibited to the Jews, was one of the consequences of this last confrontation between Rome and the Jews. The Christians did not associate with this uprising either, and subsequently showed themselves even more loyal to the Roman empire. However, the destruction of Palestinian Judaism, from which Babylonian Judaism took over, had repercussions for the fate of Christianity in Palestine. This was thrown into complete disarray and lost all its importance.

Thus disappeared one of the last Christian circles within the Roman empire which had maintained relations with Judaism.

As the gulf between Judaism and Christianity deepened, the Christians, at any rate those who lived in the Roman empire and who from now on formed the great majority of the Christian people, felt a growing need for integration within Greco-Roman civilization. We know of this integration and this aspiration, which were certainly phenomena of everyday life, only through the literary works of this period. This testimony is indirect, but the diversity of works in question confirms its solidity. These documents can be grouped into several categories: a Syrian text, the Gospel of Thomas; two texts from Alexandria in Egypt (the Second Letter of Peter, the Letter of Barnabas); two Roman texts (the Shepherd of Hermas; the homily often called II Clement); and finally, the works of the first Apologists.

Not much can be derived for our research from the Gospel of Thomas, of which we have only Greek fragments and a Coptic version. This document is in fact very difficult to date. In essentials it reproduces sayings of Jesus handed down by an autonomous tradition going back well into the first century of our era. While it is very useful for reconstructing the message of Jesus, this tradition, which went from Aramaic to Greek, and then from the oral stage to the written stage, tells us almost nothing about Christianity in the first half of the second century, since it did not undergo the same literary development as the canonical Gospels. However, it will be noted that the sayings of Jesus which appear in the Gospel of Thomas give the kingdom of God a non-eschatological definition (e.g. Sayings 3, 109 and 113). This could be coloured by the Greek mentality, which was hostile to eschatology. Furthermore, the rejection of Jewish practices of piety, namely fasting, prayer and almsgiving (e.g. Sayings 6 and 14), in it is absolute, as is the rejection of circumcision (Saying 53). As for sabbath observance, it is subject to a very free interpretation of the Old Testament rule (Saying 27). These are all Jewish practices which have disappeared from Christian circles, and that suggests a tendency of the latter to assimilate themselves to Greco-Roman society.[1]

The texts which probably come from Alexandria in Egypt reflect the same orientation. The Second Letter of Peter, which is generally dated around 130 CE, is the latest book of the New Testament. It was only accepted at a late stage, which shows that its attribution to the apostle Peter was not thought evident, despite the superscription in 1.1. In vocabulary and style it is the most elegant book in the New Testament.

Its author is a Hellenistic intellectual addressing an educated public. Granted, he quotes the Jewish scriptures abundantly, along with the writings of the intertestamental period, and energetically defends the traditional notion of the return of Christ. But the reason why this little pamphlet has to serve as an apologia for this parousia is because those to whom it is addressed are tempted to renounce the doctrine, doubtless because their Hellenization was very advanced. The heretics whom it brutally attacks in chapters 2 and 3 are also Hellenized. The Jews, of whose scriptures abundant use is made, do not appear anywhere. Judaism is an outmoded issue.[2]

The letter of Pseudo-Barnabas probably also comes from Alexandria in Egypt, even if some critics think that it comes from Syria-Palestine. It is usually dated to the second quarter of the second century. It is a work in which various influences, including Essenism, converge. Essenism can be sensed particularly in chapters 16 and 18–21, which reproduce the Manual of the Two Ways in a slightly different form from that which it has at Qumran.[3] Christianity, totally separate from Judaism, still has only an embryonic organization, to which moreover the author pays no particular attention. On the other hand, he is very concerned to safeguard the place and authority of the Scriptures, which for him are still only the books of the Old Testament. To do this he offers an allegorical interpretation of these writings which, even if it has some Jewish sources (e.g. Philo), is above all the application of Hellenistic hermeneutics to the reading of ancient literature. In short, here Hellenism is present in particular in the sphere in which Christianity most vigorously claimed the Jewish heritage. The Bible, which the Jews do not understand and which denounces their permanent revolt against the divine will, becomes the property of Christians through a systematic recourse to allegory, which is possible only because Christianity has flowed into the categories of Greek culture.[4] In Pseudo-Barnabas this paradoxical attitude takes so exclusive a turn that one can understand the reaction of those Christians who would opt for the rejection of the Old Testament (many of the Gnostics, Marcion) or for the purging of the collection, from which the 'false pericopes' were to be eliminated (the Pseudo-Clementine writings, coming from Jewish-Christian circles).

If we turn to Christian texts of Roman provenance, we first meet, around 140, the Shepherd of Hermas. The aim of this long document is to affirm the fruitfulness of repentance, which allows all believers to return to grace before God. Its author, who is otherwise unknown, presents himself as a visionary and a prophet. He is inspired by the prophetic books of the Old Testament, but above all by Jewish apocalyptic literature. However, there are also plenty of borrowings from secular Greek literature in this work, both autobiography and psychological notes which are both highly refined and of a bucolic flavour. In his very personal way, like Pseudo-Barnabas the author shows how the preferential reference to the Bible was integrated into a well-assimilated Hellenistic culture. It was this synthesis, here issuing in a sentimental moralism, that provoked the indignant reaction of the Gnostics and Marcion, guardians of a Christianity which was 'wholly other'.[5]

The homily which is often entitled the Second Letter of Clement of Rome is certainly contemporary with the Shepherd of Hermas or slightly earlier. It, too, is a vibrant exhortation to repentance. The author bases his argument on numerous quotations, some of which are borrowed from the prophetic books of the Jewish Bible, especially from Isaiah. However, most are from the letters of Paul, and above all from the sayings of the Lord Jesus as these were handed down by a tradition which largely overflowed the framework of the canonical Gospels. Apart from a very high christology which affirms the divinity of Jesus Christ,[6] this writing is characterized by a very striking conception of the antiquity of the church, which was created before the sun and moon and became visible in the flesh of Christ.[7] Thus Judaism is reduced to a kind of outmoded incident in the history of the salvation.[8] As for the pagan world, it has to be won over by preaching, but also by the assiduous practice of love of enemies.[9] The believer is invited to depart from the world and to break with the present age.[10] There is no aspiration here to become assimilated to Greco-Roman culture, but a vigorous exhortation to a presence in the world which prohibits Christians from retreating into a disincarnate spirituality.[11]

The atmosphere changes when we turn to the writings of the first Apologists. Around 125 Quadratus of Athens wrote an open letter to Hadrian; all we have of it is an extract published by Eusebius of Caesarea in his *Church History* IV, 3. In this passage the author makes the miracles of Jesus the proof that he was the saviour of the world. The rest of this letter doubtless tried to argue the cause of Christianity to the Roman authorities.

The *Apology* of Aristides, published around 145, is the earliest of the apologies the text of which has been preserved. It severely condemns the pagan cults and accuses the Jews of worshipping angels and not God himself. Only Christians offer God the appropriate worship. The best indication that they worship the true God is their moral behaviour, which is all that society could wish. They help the widow and orphan and, with the food that they save by fasting, they succour the needy. These are actions already commended by the synagogues of the Diaspora, but the Christians practise them in a more organized and wider way. In short, they behave as perfect citizens and should be treated as such.

The later Apologists, like Justin Martyr, Melito of Sardes, Athenagoras, and the anonymous author of the Letter to Diognetus, continue along the same lines, trying to dispel all the misunderstandings of Christianity in Greco-Roman society. All are moved by the desire to make Christianity acceptable to public opinion and to the Roman authorities, whether in doctrine, morality or worship. On this last point, a desire to refute the calumnies which had spread among the pagans has given us, in Justin's *First Apology*, chapters 65, 66 and 67 (around 150), a presentation of baptism, the eucharist and, more generally, the weekly liturgy of the Christian communities. Here we find many of the features of synagogue meetings, beginning with good order and a sermon which refers to a passage of scripture.[12] We are far from the disorderly enthusiasm of the churches founded by Paul. Christianity has become a respectable religion which the Greeks and Romans have no reason to reject. The disappearance of the apostolate and all missionary ministries points in the same direction. The gospel is no longer perceived as aggressive religious propaganda, but as the faith of a reasonable community.

This respectability and this aspiration to be recognized by surrounding society were not to the taste of all Christians. Three unrelated tendencies asserted themselves between 130 and 150 to defend the originality of Christianity against the slide of the great church into an increasing cultural assimilation to Greco-Roman civilization: some Jewish-Christian writers whose ideas are expressed in the Gospel of the Ebionites, the Gospel of the Hebrews and the *Kerygma Petri* (Preaching of Peter); the first Gnostic thinkers, represented in particular by Basilides; and Marcion's schism. Unfortunately the texts produced by these anti-assimilationist Christians are known only through what their opponents said about them, sometimes in inconsistent and even contradictory terms. The Preaching of Peter and the Jewish-Christian Gospels are known to us only from some quotations made from them by Clement of Alexandria in Book VI of his *Stromata* for the former and various later authors for the latter. They can certainly be said to come from Alexandria, except for the Gospel of the Ebionites, which probably comes from Jordan. The few elements of doctrine which one can discover bear witness to a Christianity firmly rooted in the Jewish heritage, with a resolute monotheism that is hard to reconcile with the christology of the great church, and also some traces of Gnostic influence. It is in the Preaching of Peter that we find the first mention of Christians as the 'third race', distinct both from the Jews and the Greeks. In these Jewish Christians there is no sign of a desire to be integrated into Greco-Roman civilization.[13] That certainly was also the case with their Aramaic-speaking brothers, of whom there were no doubt many. However, we have no knowledge of them in this period.

Basilides, the first of the great Gnostic teachers, was active between c.125 and c.155. We know that he wrote twenty-four books of exegesis of scripture, but we know his ideas only through the comments, for the most part critical, of authors like Irenaeus (c.130–c.200), Hippolytus (c.160–236), Clement of Alexandria (active between 180 and 203), and Epiphanius (367–404). These ideas were taken up by his son and disciple Isidore, and then by a whole theological school. Basilides professed the absolute transcendence of God, from whom Thought, then the Word, then Prudence, Wisdom and Power had emanated. From there had come the angels and the powers which constituted the first heaven, and then the 365 heavens which separated God from the group of the lowest angels who had created the world and had distributed the peoples among them. Yahweh, the angel of Israel, was a quarrelsome and authoritarian figure who had sowed disorder and whose people were constantly aggressive. So God had had to intervene, which he had done by sending his Thought into the world as Christ. Human beings had supposed that they could rid themselves of this by crucifying it, but in reality it was Simon of Cyrene who had undergone execution under the guise of Christ, whereas Christ mocked his Jewish adversaries. This gigantic mythological edifice, certainly inspired by pre-Christian Gnostic myths, was characterized at every level except the highest by ignorance; this led each of the intermediary beings to regard themselves as the supreme God. Salvation was brought by knowledge (Gnosis) revealed by Christ and by inspired teachers. With this 'gnosis' evil was overcome, since it was not the work of the wicked Yahweh. There remained the problem of the suffering of the righteous, which Basilides also attributed to the action of Yahweh, but which had to be experienced as an expiation for the sins of each believer.

The result of this grandiose scheme was a complete break not only with contemporary Judaism but also with the Jewish heritage, apart from scripture, the meaning of which had to be discovered by a wide-spread use of allegory. Despite this borrowing from Hellenism, Basilides did not favour an alignment of Christianity with Greco-Roman civilization. The Christian's need to endure suffering and martyrdom forbade any accommodation with the current morality. To be a Christian was not to seek tolerance or recognition from the world, but to keep one's distance from it in order not to succumb to a mediocrely optimistic morality which would empty the existence of the believer of its tragic content.[14]

Marcion (c.85–c.160) did not have the intellectual ambition of the Gnostic teachers, but his influence on the Christian milieu was perhaps deeper than theirs. He was born at Sinope, on the Anatolian coast of the Black Sea, in a Christian family. A shipbuilder and merchant, he travelled often on business, readily speaking on religious questions, which involved him in a still famous conflict with Polycarp, bishop of Smyrna. Around 135 he settled in Rome, where he became a member of the church and gave it a considerable donation. This ensured that he had a great influence on Christian circles in the capital. Some years later he published a theological work, *The Antitheses*, in which he professed that the God of Jesus had nothing to do with the Yahweh of the Old Testament, an ignorant, brutal and materialistic deity. Jesus himself was not the Messiah announced by the prophets, the earthly liberator of the Jewish people, but the Son of the Unknown God mentioned by Paul in Acts 17.23. So the gospel was the totally new offer of a grace intended for all human beings. The scripture which attested this incomparable revelation was not the Jewish Bible but a new collection made up of the Gospel of Luke, stripped of its first two chapters and the accounts of the appearances of the Risen Christ, and the corpus of the letters of Paul, purged of references to the Old Testament and not including the Pastoral Epistles. In 144 Marcion was expelled from the church of Rome; he launched out on very active missionary campaigns and founded numerous churches which practised a very austere morality, including the renunciation of sex and family life, as a preparation for martyrdom. The repudiation of the material world and of evil represented an absolute rejection of any accommodation with Greco-Roman culture and also a complete break with the Jewish heritage.

These three manifestations of the rejection of assimilation to the surrounding culture did not impress the Christian majority. However, they weighed heavily on the development of Christianity, forcing the great church to organize better, to define and defend its faith better, and to be more precise about what it recognized as holy scripture. As has often been noted, the challenges mentioned above largely contributed to the spread of the monarchical episcopate throughout the great church and the disappearance of collegial trends. It also led to the final redaction and dissemination of the Apostles' Creed, together with the first theological works (Justin, Irenaeus and Clement of Alexandria), and finally to the formation of a canon of scripture including both the Old and New Testaments, even if the precise limits of this twofold collection were not fixed until the end of antiquity. In short, Christianity, which discovered its own identity around 100 CE, sought to insert itself into the society where the majority of its members had chosen to establish themselves and engaged in a vast internal debate on how this was to be done. By virtue of this, it can be said to have been emancipated from its progenitor, Judaism, and before 150 entered on adulthood, when it had to take its own destiny in hand.

Conclusion

The first century of the history of Christianity, which people often set out to present as the simple beginnings of the church, a religious institution proud of its stability and its continuity, was in fact marked by several turning points. These were both unexpected and decisive: the premature death of Jesus, the appearances of the Risen Christ, the establishment of the disciples in Jerusalem, the upheaval caused by the Hellenists, Paul's break with the mainstream church, the terrible storm of the 60s, the relaunching of Judaism by Johanan ben Zakkai and his disciples, the exclusion of the *minim* from the synagogues around 90–100 and the opening at the beginning of the second century of the great debate on the integration of Christianity within Greco-Roman society. I hope that I have shown that the collective consciousness of the Christians, still limited to their attachment to the Risen Christ during the first years, was gradually formed and enriched in the course of these successive shocks. Initially messianic Jews, they progressively became aware of their originality over against Judaism. Aramaic-speaking to begin with, they discovered Greek culture, and the majority of them opted for this new milieu. On the frontier between the Parthian and Roman empires, many of them turned towards the latter and neglected the possibilities opened up by the strong Jewish settlements in Mesopotamia, thus creating a gulf between a somewhat languishing Eastern Christianity and a Western Christianity which was dynamic, but closed to the East.[1]

With the help of circumstances, this group, long dominated by its original milieu, came to understand better and better that it had an autonomous personality. It began to spread its wings, towards the amazing destiny of becoming the religion of the Roman empire and then the religion of Europe. Between 125 and 150 nothing yet made it possible to predict this impressive future. But the decisive choices had already been made. Christianity, which had emerged from its Jewish framework after three or four generations of growth in this protective milieu, from now on stood alone in confronting the world around it. As an adult, it had gained a full knowledge of itself. As a young adult, it still had the presumption shown by the Apologists and the intrepidity of the confessors who rejected all concessions. Its childhood was certainly at an end. It was ready to confront the storms of maturity, which looked like being fierce ones.

Bibliography

Some Books on the Beginnings of Christianity

I shall limit myself to a small number of important titles which have appeared over the last fifty years on the general history of the first century of Christianity. For monographs on particular problems or particular figures see the Notes.

P. Carrington, *The Early Christian Church* (2 vols.), Cambridge: Cambridge University Press 1957

H. Conzelmann, *A History of Primitive Christianity*, London: Darton, Longman and Todd 1971

J. Daniélou and H. Marrou, *The Christian Centuries: A New History of the Catholic Church*, Vol.1: *The First Six Hundred Years*, London: Darton, Longman and Todd 1964

J.D.G. Dunn, *The Partings of the Ways*, London: SCM Press 1991

Eusebius of Caesarea, *Ecclesiastical History*, Harmondsworth: Penguin Books 1965

W.H.C. Frend, *The Rise of Christianity*, London: Darton, Longman and Todd 1984

M. Goguel, *Jesus*, London: Allen and Unwin 1933

—, *The Birth of Christianity*, London: Allen and Unwin 1962

—, *The Primitive Church*, London: Allen and Unwin 1964

L. Goppelt, *Les Origines de l'Eglise. Christianisme et judaisme aux deux premiers siècles*, Paris: Payot, 1961

H. Kraft, *Die Entstehung des Christentums*, Darmstadt: Wissenschaftliche Buchgesellschaft 1981

D. Marguerat (ed.), *Le Déchirement. Juifs et chrétiens au premier siècle*, Le Monde du Bible, Geneva: Labor et Fides 1996

J.M. Robinson and H. Koester, *Trajectories through Early Christianity*, Philadelphia: Fortress Press 1971

M. Simon and A. Benoit, *Le Judaisme et le christianisme antique d'Antiochus Epiphane à Constantin*, Paris: Presses Universitaires de France 1968, ⁴1994

M. Simon, *La Civilization de l'Antiquité et le Christianisme*, Paris: Arthaud 1972

S.G. Wilson, *Related Strangers, Jews and Christians 20–170 CE*, Minneapolis: Fortress Press 1995

Notes

1. *Judaism at the Beginning of Our Era*

1. More information about the content of this chapter can be found in E.P. Sanders, *Judaism: Practice and Belief, 63 BCE–66 CE*, London and Philadelphia 1992; Lester Grabbe, *Judaism from Cyrus to Hadrian*, London and Minneapolis 1994.

2. *John the Baptist and Jesus of Nazareth*

1. Mark 1.1–8 par.; Mark 1.9–11 par.; Mark 2.18 par.; Mark 6.14–16 par.; Mark 8.28 par.; Mark 11.29–33 par.
2. Mark 1.14 par.; Mark 6.17–29 par.; Mark 9.9–13 par.
3. Matt. 11.2–19 par.
4. Matt. 21.32.
5. Luke 1.5–80; 11.1.
6. John 1.6–8,15; 1.19–37; 3.22–4.3; 5.33–36; 10.40–41.
7. Acts 1.5, 22; 10.37; 11.16; 13.24; 18.24–26; 10.1–8.
8. Mark 2.18 par.
9. Luke 3.10–12.
10. Mal.3.22–24.
11. Mark 6.17–29.
12. Matt. 11.2–19.
13. Matt. 3.14; Luke 1.44.
14. Mark 6.29.
15. Acts 18.24–26; 19.1–8.
16. Cf. especially John 3.22–36.
17. Clementine Recognitions I,60; Ephraem, *Evangeliorum Concordantiae Expositio*; some passages from the *Ginza*, the scripture of the Mandaean sect.
18. For John the Baptist and his milieu and his attitude to Jesus see e.g. Maurice Goguel, *Au seuil de l'Évangile, Jean-Baptiste*, Paris 1928; Jean Daniélou, *The Work of John the Baptist*, Baltimore 1966; Charles H. Scobie, *John the Baptist*, London 1964; Laurent Guyénot, *Le roi sans Prophète, l'enquête historique sur la relation entre Jésus et Jean Baptiste*, no place 1996.
19. In 1906 Albert Schweitzer gave a penetrating account of the disputes surrounding the Lives of Jesus (English *The Quest of the Historical Jesus*,

[3]1950; the title of the first German edition was *Von Reimarus zu Wrede*). The confrontations have continued since then.

20. Cf. Étienne Trocmé, *Jesus and His Contemporaries*, London 1973. Unfortunately, the innumerable Lives of Jesus which flood the market prefer the picturesque to the commonsensical.

21. The Egyptian Jesus of Philippe d'Aulan, *La Parole de Jésus*, Saint-Michel de Boulogne 1996, based on a very personal interpretation of the Gospel of Thomas, has no historical probability.

22. John 3.26.
23. John 3.22; 4.1–2.
24. Mark 1.14 par.
25. Mark 1.15; Luke 17.20–21.
26. Mark 1.15. That is how this phrase should be understood.
27. Mark 6.30–45 par.; 8.1–10 par.
28. Mark 1.22.
29. Matt. 5.17–48.
30. Matt. 5.3–12.
31. Mark 6.33–34.
32. Mark 12.13–27 par.
33. Mark 11.15–18, 27–33; 12.1–12, 28–40 par.
34. Mark 14.36.
35. Cf. Mark 2.10, 28; 8.31, 38; 9.9; 12,31; 10.33, 45; 13.26; 14.21, 41, 62 par.
36. Mark 11.15–19 par.
37. Étienne Trocmé, *The Passion as Liturgy*, London 1983, has demonstrated this by analysing the accounts of the Passion, which are still too neglected by authors who write on this subject, like Simon Légasse, *Le Procès de Jésus* (2 vols), Paris 1994–1996 (English translation of Vol.1, *The Trial of Jesus*, London 1997).

3. The First Church of Jerusalem

1. John 21.2–3.
2. Luke 24.17–21.
3. Cf. Acts 10.40–41.
4. Matt. 28.9–10, 18–20; Luke 24.13–53; John 20.14–29; 21.1–23.
5. Acts 1.3–11.
6. Acts 9.1–19; 22.6–16; 26.12–18.
7. Gal. 1.15–17; I Cor. 9.1; 15.8.
8. As I think I have demonstrated in my *Le 'Livre des Actes' et l'histoire*, Paris 1957, 175–9.
9. Matt. 28.9–10; John 20.14–18.
10. Matt. 28.1–7; Mark 16.1–8; Luke 24.1–11; John 20.1–2, 11–13.
11. Cf. Mark 16.8; Luke 24.11.
12. I Cor. 15.5; Luke 24.34.
13. I Cor. 15.7.
14. I Cor. 15.5.

15. I Cor. 15.7.
16. I Cor. 15.6.
17. Matt. 28.16–20; John 21.
18. Luke 24.13–32; Acts 9.1–19; 22.6–16; 26.12–18.
19. Acts 1.9.
20. Acts 1.13–14.
21. Gal. 1.18–19.
22. Acts 4.34–37.
23. Acts 5.1–11.
24. Cf. Mark 3.13–19 par.
25. Cf. Matt. 19.28 par.
26. Community Rule VIII, 1–4.
27. Cf. Christian Grappe, *D'un Temple à l'autre. Pierre et l'Église primitive de Jérusalem*, Paris 1992, 51–73.
28. Acts 6.1.
29. Acts 2.46; 3.1.
30. Acts 2.46.
31. Acts 2.38–41.
32. Acts 2.42.
33. C.H. Dodd, *According to the Scriptures*, London 1952.
34. Mark 12.28–34 par.
35. Matt. 5.17–48 par.
36. Luke 10.29–37.
37. Rudolf Bultmann, *History of the Synoptic Tradition*, Oxford ²1968.
38. Acts 2.41; 4.4.
39. Acts 9.1–2, 10, 19; Acts 9.30–43; Acts 9.32.
40. Acts 9.31.
41. Acts 6.8; 8.5–7.
42. Marcel Simon, *Saint Stephen and the Hellenists in the Primitive Church*, London 1958; Martin H. Scharlemann, *Stephen, A Singular Saint*, Rome 1968.
43. Acts 6.13–14; 7.46–53.
44. Acts 7.57–60.
45. Acts 8.1–3.
46. Cf. John 18.15.
47. Oscar Cullmann, *The Johannine Circle*, London 1976; J.D. Kaestli, J.M. Poffet and J. Zumstein (eds.), *La Communauté johannique et son histoire, la trajectoire de l'évangile de Jean aux deux premiers siècles*, Geneva 1990.
48. Acts 12.1–2.
49. Acts 12.3–4.
50. Acts 12.5–11.
51. Acts 12.17.
52. Acts 15.7–11.
53. The best study of St Peter continues to be Oscar Cullmann, *Peter: Disciple, Apostle, Martyr*, London 1953; cf. also Grappe, *D'un Temple à l'autre* (n.27), 139–286.
54. Acts 21.18.

55. Gal. 1.18–19.
56. Gal. 2.1; cf. Gal. 1.18.
57. Gal. 2.9.
58. Gal. 2.11ff.
59. For James, see the excellent study by Pierre-Antoine Bernheim, *James, Brother of Jesus*, London 1997.
60. Eusebius, *Church History* II, 1, 2, who quotes Clement of Alexandria; Jerome, *De viris illustribus* II, etc.
61. Acts 1.14; I Cor. 9.5; cf. Jude 1.
62. Matt. 1.1; Luke 1.32; 3.31; Rom. 1.3; I Timothy 2.8; Rev. 5.5; 22.16.
63. Eusebius, *Church History* III, 11, 1; IV, 22,4.
64. Eusebius, *Church History* III, 20,6; III, 32,6.
65. Mark 12.35–37 par.; John 7.42.
66. Mark 3.20–35 and its partial parallels; Mark 6.1–6 par.; John 7.2–9.
67. Acts 11.30; 15.2.
68. Eusebius, *Church History* II, 23,4–18.
69. Acts 15.13–21.
70. Gal. 2.1–10.
71. Cf. Gal. 2.1–10; Rom. 15.25–27.
72. Acts 11.22–24.
73. Acts 11.27–29.
74. Acts 15.1–33. We shall be returning to this account below, 48–50.
75. Gal. 2.14ff.
76. Gal. 2.11–13.
77. Gal. 1.6–9; 3.1; 4.17; 5.7–12; 6.12–13; Phil. 3.2, 18–19; II Cor. 3.1; 5.12; 10.12; 11.4–5, 12–15, 18–23; 12.11.
78. Rom. 15.23.
79. Rom. 15.25–32.
80. Acts 20 and 21.
81. Gal. 2.10ff.
82. Acts 15.23.
83. Cf. M. Simon, 'De l'observance rituelle à l'ascèse, recherches sur le Décret apostolique', *Revue de l'historie des religions* CXCIII.1, Paris 1978, 27–104, reprinted in *Le Christianisme antique et son contexte religieux. Scripta varia*, Tübingen 1981, II, 725–802.
84. Josephus, *Jewish Antiquities* XX, 9,1.
85. Eusebius, *Church History* II, 23.
86. We shall be returning to these events below, 79–80.
87. Eusebius, *Church History* III, 11,1.
88. Eusebius, *Church History* III, 5,3.
89. Cf. below, 80.

4. *The Spread of the 'Hellenists'*

1. Acts 8.1.
2. Acts 8.4.
3. Acts 6.5.

4. Acts 8.5.
5. Acts 8.6–7.
6. Acts 8.8.
7. Acts 8.6.
8. Acts 8.12.
9. Acts 8.9.
10. Acts 8.10.
11. Acts 8.13.
12. Acts 8.14.
13. Acts 8.15–16.
14. Acts 8.26–40.
15. Acts 8.38–39.
16. Cf. Acts 10.44–48.
17. Cf. Acts 8.18–24.
18. Acts 8.26–39.
19. Cf. I Kings 18 and especially v.12.
20. Acts 8.40.
21. Cf. Acts 9.32–36; 10.1–48.
22. Acts 21.8–14.
23. Acts 21.15–16.
24. Acts 11.19.
25. Acts 11.20–21. A large number of ancient manuscripts have a variant *Hellenistas* rather than the reading *Hellenas*, which would seem preferable and is equally well attested.
26. Acts 11.22–24; 13.1.
27. Acts 11.25–26; 9.26–28.
28. Acts 13.1.
29. Acts 11.25.
30. Acts 11.26; 13.1.
31. Acts 13.1–3.
32. Gal. 2.12–13.
33. Acts 13 to 15.
34. Acts 8.14–24.
35. Acts 9.32–43.
36. Gal. 2.11.
37. Acts 8.25.
38. Acts 10.1–11.18.
39. Acts 15.7–11.
40. I Cor. 1.12; 3.22.
41. I Cor. 9.5.
42. I Peter 1.1
43. I Peter 5.13. For the interpretation of this passage cf. O. Cullmann, *Peter: Disciple, Apostle*, Martyr, London 1953, 82–6.
44. Acts 11.21–24.
45. Acts 13–14; 15.36–39; I Cor. 9.6.
46. Gal. 1.17.
47. Acts 8.32–35.

48. Acts 7.2–53.
49. Acts 6.7; cf. 21.20.
50. Acts 7.55–56.
51. Acts 7.52.
52. Acts 7.55–56.
53. Cf. Matt. 25.31–46.
54. Acts 7.47–50.
55. I have made a contribution to this debate which does not seem to me to have been superseded, in Étienne Trocmé, *La Formation de l'Évangile selon Marc*, Paris 1963, esp. 169–203.
56. Mark 8.31–32; 9.31; 10.32–34.
57. Mark 8.32–33; 10.35–40.
58. Mark 3.20–35; 6.1–6.
59. Cf. Mark 7.3–4; 12.42.
60. Mark 8.34.
61. Rom. 1.16–17.
62. Mark 1.27; 4.41; 7.37; 9.32; 10.32; 14.3; 16.8.
63. Mark 1.16–20; 2.14; 6.7–13; 8.34–35; 10.17–31.
64. Mark 10.42–44. No one has shown this better than Kenzo Tagawa in his fine book *Miracles et Évangile*, Paris 1966.
65. Mark 10.45.
66. Mark 8.35.
67. Mark 7.1–23.
68. Mark 2.18–20.
69. Mark 2.23–3.6.
70. Mark 10.1–12.
71. Mark 11.12–25.
72. Mark 1.44; 2.25–28; 7.10; 10.5–9; 10.17–19, 28–33.
73. Cf. Mark 5.1–20; 7.24–30, 31–37; 13.10.
74. Mark 1.14–15; 6.35–45; 8.1–9.
75. Mark 1.16–20; 2.13–14; 3.13–19; 6.6–13; 8.34–9.1; 9.33–50; 10.17–31; 10.35–45.
76. Mark 8.38.
77. Acts 21.3–14.

5. Paul, The First Steps

1. There are innumerable biographies of Paul. J. Knox, *Chapters in a Life of Paul*, Nashville and London 1960, is a classic; more recently see E.P. Sanders, *Paul*, Oxford 1991; J. Murphy-O'Connor, *Paul. A Critical Life*, Oxford 1996.
2. Acts 22.28.
3. Acts 16.37; 22.25–29; 23.27.
4. Acts of Paul and Thecla 3.
5. Gal. 4.13.
6. II Cor. 12.7–9.
7. Philemon 9.

8. Cf. II Cor. 11.23–29.
9. Phil. 3.5.
10. Ibid.
11. Phil. 3.6; cf. Gal. 1.14.
12. Acts 23.6; cf. 26.5.
13. Acts 22.3.
14. Cf. Acts 21.40.
15. Acts 7.58; 8.1.
16. Acts 8.3.
17. I Cor. 15.9; Gal. 1.13–23; Phil. 3.6; cf. Acts 26.9–11.
18. Gal. 1.14; Phil. 3.6.
19. Cf. Acts 22.3.
20. Rom. 15.31.
21. Acts 9.1–2.
22. Acts 9.3ff.
23. Cf. also Phil. 3.12.
24. I Cor. 15.8–9.
25. Acts 9.3–19; 22.6–21; 26.12–18.
26. A detailed demonstration of this analysis of the three accounts of the event on the Damascus road can be found in my *Le 'Livre des Actes' et l'histoire*, Paris 1957, 174–8.
27. Rom. 11.1–5; cf. I Kings 19.10, 14, 18.
28. Rom. 11.13–15, 25–27.
29. Gal. 1.17.
30. II Cor. 11.32–33.
31. Acts 9.23–25.
32. II Cor. 11.30–31.
33. Gal. 1.18.
34. I Cor. 7.10–11; 11.23–25; 15.3–7.
35. Gal. 1.19.
36. Acts 9.28.
37. Acts 9.27; cf. Acts 4.36–37.
38. Acts 9.29–30.
39. Acts 18.3.
40. Acts 13.1.
41. Acts 11.26.
42. Acts 11.29–30; 12.25.
43. Acts 11.28.
44. Acts 13.2–3.
45. Acts 13.4.
46. Acts 4.36.
47. Acts 13.5.
48. Acts 12.25.
49. Cf. also Acts 12.12.
50. Acts 13.6.
51. Acts 13.6–12.
52. Acts 8.18–24.

53. Acts 13.13.
54. Cf. Acts 15.37–40.
55. Cf. Gal. 4.12–13.
56. This is the thesis of Marie-Françoise Baslez, *Saint Paul*, Paris 1991, 125–7.
57. Cf. Acts 11.30; 15.2, 4, 6, 22, 23; 21.18.
58. Acts 14.4, 14.
59. Acts 14.24–28.
60. Cf. Acts 15.36–40.
61. Acts 15.
62. Gal. 2.1–10.
63. Acts 15.2.
64. Gal. 2.1.
65. Gal. 1.18–24.
66. Cf. Gal. 1.15–18.
67. The precise chronology of Paul's life is so complex that whole works have been devoted to this question alone. See especially Robert Jewett, *Dating Paul's Life*, London 1979, and Gerd Lüdemann, *Paul, Apostle to the Gentiles. Studies in Chronology*, Philadelphia and London 1984.
68. Gal. 2.3–5.
69. Acts 10.9–16.
70. Cf. Acts 15.7–11.
71. Gal. 2.9–10.

6. Paul, Flight Forward

1. Gal. 2.1–10.
2. Gal. 2.11–13.
3. Gal. 2.14ff.
4. Acts 15.36–39.
5. Acts 18.22–23; cf. 59 below.
6. Acts 15.40.
7. Though this thesis is accepted by only a minority of critics, it has found eminent defenders, of whom Ernest Renan is the best known. It is worth following, despite the objections summarized by Pierre Bonnard, *L'Épître de Saint Paul aux Galates*, Neuchâtel ¹1953, ²1972, 10–12.
8. Gal. 1.6.
9. Gal 1.7.
10. Gal. 1.8–9.
11. Gal. 2.7–9.
12. Gal. 2.16–21.
13. Gal. 3.1–5.
14. Gal. 3.6–22.
15. Gal. 3.23–4.7.
16. Gal. 4.21–31.
17. Gal. 5.12–6.10.
18. Gal. 6.11.
19. Gal. 4.22.

20. Acts 15.36, 41; 16.1–2.
21. Acts 16.4.
22. Acts 15.13ff.
23. Gal. 2.7–9.
24. Acts 16.1–3.
25. Gal. 2.3–5.
26. Acts 15.41–16.5.
27. Acts 16.6–12.
28. II Cor. 2.12–13; Acts 20.6–12.
29. Rom. 1.9–13; 15.22–24, 28, 29.
30. II Cor. 11.8; Phil 4.15–16.
31. Acts 20.6.
32. Acts 16.10.
33. I think that I have demonstrated this in my *Le 'Livre des Actes' et l'histoire*, Paris 1957, 122–44.
34. Acts 16.16–18.
35. Acts 16.19–34.
36. Acts 16.35–40.
37. Acts 16.21.
38. Acts 16.39.
39. Acts 17.1.
40. Acts 17.2–4.
41. Acts 17.5–13.
42. Acts 20.1–2, 3, 6.
43. I Thess. 2.17–3.10; Phil. 1.25–26; Acts 19.21.
44. Phil. 2.19–30; Acts 19.22; I Thess. 3.1–6.
45. Phil. 1.3–8; 2.12; 4.1.
46. Phil. 4.10–20; II Cor. 11.8–9.
47. II Cor. 8.1–5.
48. Cf. Bertil Gärtner, *The Areopagus Speech and Natural Revelation*, Uppsala 1955.
49. Acts 18.1–11.
50. Acts 18.12–17.
51. Acts 18.18.
52. Num. 6.9–18.
53. Cf. Gal. 2.7–9.

7. Paul, Church Leader

1. Acts 18.23.
2. Acts 19.1.
3. Acts 18.24–26; 19.1–4.
4. Acts 19.9.
5. Acts 19.10.
6. Cf. Acts 20.31.
7. Acts 19.10.
8. Cf. Col. 1.7; 4.13,15; Rev. 3.14–22.

9. Acts 19.11–20.
10. I Cor. 15.32; II Cor. 1.8.
11. Phil. 1.7, 13–14.
12. Acts 19.21 – 20.1.
13. Phil. 3.2ff., 18–19.
14. Acts 18.24–28.
15. I Cor. 1.12; 3.4.
16. I Cor. 3.6.
17. I Cor. 4.15.
18. I Cor. 16.12.
19. I Cor. 4.17; 16.10–11.
20. I Cor. 1.12; 3.22; 9.5.
21. I Cor. 9.1–18; II Cor. 11.7–10.
22. II Cor. 10.1–10; 11.6.
23. II Cor. 11.22.
24. I Cor. 9.19–27; II Cor. 10.13–18; 11.23–29.
25. II Cor. 12.1–6.
26. II Cor. 11.30–33; 12.7–10.
27. II Cor. 11.13–15.
28. II Cor. 2.5–11.
29. II Cor. 13.2.
30. For this point see the works of Gerd Theissen and in particular his fine article 'Soziale Schichtung in der korinthischen Gemeinde', *Zeitschrift für die neutestamentliche Wissenschaft* 65, 1974, 233–72.
31. I Cor. 2.
32. Cf. Mark 12.18 par.; Acts 23.8.
33. Cf. Gal. 3.26–29; II Cor. 5.17; Rom. 1.17; 5.1–11.
34. I Cor. 15.1–11.
35. I Cor. 15.20.
36. I Cor. 15.12–34.
37. I Cor. 15.35–36.
38. See for example Pierre Grelot, 'La Résurrection de Jésus et son arrière-plan biblique et juif', and Maurice Carrez, 'L'herméneutique paulinienne de la résurrection', in *La Résurrection du Christ et l'exégèse moderne*, Paris 1969, 17–53 and 55–73 respectively.
39. I Cor. 7.1.
40. I Cor. 8.1.
41. I Cor. 12.1.
42. I Cor. 5.1–13.
43. I Cor 6.1–11.
44. I Cor. 6.12–20.
45. I Cor. 11.2–34 and ch.14.
46. The best account of Paul's ideas in this sphere is to be found in Max-Alain Chevallier, *Souffle de Dieu, le Saint-Esprit dans le Nouveau Testament* II, Paris 1990, 265–407.
47. I Cor. 12.
48. I Cor. 13.

49. I Cor. 14.
50. I Cor. 14.34–35.
51. Cf. I Tim. 2.11–15.
52. Gal. 3.28.
53. I Cor. 11.2–16.
54. I Cor. 11.17–34.
55. I Cor. 16.1–4; II Cor. 8; 9; Rom. 15.25–38.
56. Cf. Acts 20.4–6.
57. Cf. II Cor. 1.8.
58. Cf. Rom. 15.23.
59. Acts 20.4–21.14.
60. Phil. 1.1.
61. I Tim. 3.1–7; Titus 1.7–9. This term, which means 'inspectors', has led to the English 'bishops'.
62. I Tim. 3.8–13.
63. Titus 1.5–6.
64. I Cor. 1.1; II Cor. 1.1; Gal. 1.1, etc.
65. I Cor. 9.1–21; 15.9; II Cor. 12.12; I Thess. 2.7.
66. I Cor. 15.9.
67. I Cor. 9.3–18.
68. I Cor. 7.25.
69. I Cor. 7.10–11;14.37.
70. I Cor. 7.40; 14.18; 15.51; II Cor. 12.1–10; Gal. 1.11–12.
71. I Cor. 4.16; 7.7–8; 11.1; Gal. 4.12; Phil. 1.29–30; 4.9; I Thess. 1.6; II Thess. 3.6–9.
72. I Cor. 2.1–5; 3.6–10; 4.14–15; II Cor. 3.1–3; 6.13; 10.14–16; 12.14; Gal. 4.19; I Thess. 2.7–11.
73. I Cor. 4.14–21; II Cor. 2.3–4; 6.11–13; 7.2–15; 11.2–3,12; 12.14–15, 19–21; Gal. 3.1; 4.12–20; Phil. 1.7–11; 2.12–17; 4.1, 10–18; I Thess. 2.5–12, 17–20; 3.6–13; II Thess. 2.13–17.
74. I Cor. 1.10; 3.16–17; 5.11–13; 6.7; 8.7–13; 10.32; 11.20–22, 33–34; 12.12–27; 13.1–13; 14.26–33; II Cor. 2.5–9; Gal. 3.26–28; 5.13–15, 22–25; 6.1–10; Phil. 1.27–30; 2.1–5; I Thess. 3.12; 4.9–12; 5.12–15; II Thess. 3.6, 13–15.
75. Acts 20.4–21.16.
76. Acts 20.18–35.
77. Acts 21.16.
78. Acts 21.18.

8. *Paul, Theologian and Martyr*

1. Cf. Acts 17.1–8, 13; 18.4–17; 19.8–9.
2. Acts 20.2.
3. Rom. 1.1–15.
4. Rom. 15.14–33; ch.16 is an appendix, unrelated to the body of the letter.
5. Rom. 15.23–24, 28, 32.
6. Cf. Suetonius, *Claudius* 25,4, who speaks of disputes between Jews in

Rome *impulsore Christo*.

7. Rom. 1.7.
8. Cf. vv.1, 4, 5, 16, 23.
9. For a slightly different analysis of Paul's motives for writing to the Christians in Rome cf. the interesting study by Alexander J.M. Wedderburn, *The Reasons for Romans*, Edinburgh 1988.
10. Among the works devoted to the thought expressed in the letter to the Romans see especially the commentary by John Ziesler, *Paul's Letter to the Romans*, London and Philadelphia 1989, and the monograph by Halvon Moxnes, *Theology in Conflict, Studies in Paul's Understanding of God in Romans*, Leiden 1980.
11. Rom. 2.14–15, 26–27.
12. Rom. 2.28–29.2.
13. Rom. 3.21–26.
14. Rom. 3.27–5.11.
15. Rom. 5.12–21.
16. Rom. 6.1–7.6.
17. Rom. 7.7–25.
18. Rom. 8.1–39.
19. Rom. 12–15.13.
20. Paul's thought has been studied hundreds of time. I find J. Christiaan Beker, *Paul the Apostle: The Triumph of God in Life and Thought*, Edinburgh 1990, and Daniel Patte, *Paul, His Faith and the Power of the Gospel*, Philadelphia 1983, particularly illuminating.
21. Acts 28.15.
22. Acts 28.17–23.
23. Cf. I Clement 5.4–7.
24. Rom. 1.7, 15.
25. Acts 21.26–36.
26. Acts 25.13–26.32.
27. Acts 27.1–28.15.
28. II Cor. 11.25.
29. Acts 28.16–31.
30. Acts 28.15.
31. Acts 28.30–31.
32. I Clement 5.
33. Acts of Peter 1.3.
34. Even the very cautious reconstruction attempted by Marie-Françoise Baslez, *Saint Paul*, Paris 1991, 277–96, seems somewhat adventurous.
35. I Clement 5.

9. *The Great Crisis of the 60s*

1. Cf. above, 27.
2. Eusebius, *Church History* II, 23,4–18.
3. Josephus, *Jewish Antiquities* XX, 9,1.
4. Eusebius, *Church History* IV, 22, 4, who again cites Hegesippus; cf.

Church History III, 21, 1.

5. Eusebius, *Church History* III, 32,1–6.
6. Eusebius, *Church History* III, 20,6; III, 32, 6.
7. Eusebius, *Church History* IV, 22, 4–6.
8. Eusebius, *Church History* IV, 22, 4–6.
9. Cf. Josephus, *Jewish War* IV, 5,4.
10. Eusebius, *Church History* III, 5, 3.
11. Eusebius, *Demonstratio Evangelica* III, 5,10.
12. Cf. above, 32–3.
13. I Peter 1.1.
14. Cf. O. Cullmann, *Peter: Disciple, Apostle, Martyr*, London 1953, 70–152.
15. Tacitus, *Annals* XV, 44.
16. Tacitus, *Annals* XLIV, 4–9.
17. Cf. Jacob Neusner, *Life of Johanan ben Zakkai*, Leiden 1970.
18. John 9.22; 12.42.
19. The exact scope of the conclusions of the Jamnia assembly remain a matter of dispute, but their importance is evident. Cf. e.g. Peter Schäfer, *Histoire des Juifs dans l'Antiquité*, Paris 1989, 166–8.

10. *The Christian Counter-Offensive*

1. For this letter cf. Sophie Laws, *Commentary on the Epistle of James*, London and New York 1980.
2. James 1.1; 2.1.
3. James 2.14–26.
4. James 2.1–13; 3.1–18.
5. Cf. James 4.13–17; 5.1–6.
6. Cf. in particular 1.13–18, 27; 2.5; 4.4–10.
7. Cf. 2.8–13.
8. From the vast literature on the Gospel of Matthew, in English see especially G. Bornkamm, G. Barth and H.J. Held, *Tradition and Interpretation in Matthew*, London 1963; E. Schweizer, *Good News according to Matthew*, Nashville and London 1976; J.D. Kingsbury, *Matthew as Story*, Philadelphia ²1988; W.D. Davies, *The Setting of the Sermon on the Mount*, Cambridge 1963.
9. Matt. 23.8–12.
10. Matt. 5.3–12.
11. Matt. 28.18–20.

11. *A New Dawn for Paul's Heirs*

1. Cf. James 2.1–3.18.
2. Luke 4.24–27.
3. Luke 7.1–10; 8.26–37; 17.11–19.
4. Luke 10.29–37.
5. Luke 9.51–56; 17.11.
6. Mark 7.17–23; 10.2–9.
7. Cf. Acts 2.5.

8. Acts 8.
9. Acts 11.19–21.
10. Acts 10.
11. Acts 9–28.
12. Research into Luke-Acts has not paid much attention to an analysis of this plea. However, one can find some references to studies which touch on this question in François Bovon, *Luc le théologien, vingt-cinq ans de recherches (1950–1975)*, Neuchâtel 1978, 342–62. See also P.H. Mueller, 'Die jüdische Entscheidung gegen Jesus nach der Apostelgeschichte', in J. Kremer (ed.), *Les Actes des Apôtres*, Gembloux and Louvain 1979, 523–31.
13. I and II Timothy; Titus.
14. Cf. Acts 16.1; 17.14–15; 18.5; 19.22; 20.4; Rom. 16.21; I Cor. 4.17; 16.10; II Cor. 1.1, 19; Phil. 1.1; 2.19; Col.1.1; I Thess. 1.1; 3.2,6; II Thess. 1.1; Philemon 1.
15. II Cor. 2.13; 7.6, 13, 14; 8.6, 16, 23; 12.8; Gal. 2.1, 3.
16. I Tim. 3.1–7; Titus 1.7–9.
17. I Tim. 5.17–21; Titus 1.5–6.
18. I Tim. 3.8–13.
19. I Tim. 5.3–10.
20. I Tim. 2.8–15; 5.11–16; 6.1–2, 17–19; Titus 2.1–10; 3.1–2.
21. Titus 3.9.
22. I Timothy 1.4; Titus 1.14.
23. I Tim. 4.3.
24. II Tim. 2.18.
25. I Tim. 1.7, 10.
26. Cf. I Tim. 4.6–7.
27. Hardly any progress has been made on the Pastoral Epistles since Maurice Goguel, *Introduction au Nouveau Testament* IV/2, Paris 1926, 276–651, and Ceslas Spicq, *Saint Paul: les épîtres pastorales*, Paris 1947.
28. Cf. Eph. 1.1.
29. Eph. 4.11–13.
30. Cf. the commentary on this letter by R. Schnackenburg, *The Epistle to the Ephesians*, Edinburgh 1991.
31. Cf. I Cor. 5.9; II Cor. 2.3–4.
32. There are some interesting comments on the formation of the collection of Paul's letters in Robert M. Grant, *The Formation of the New Testament*, London 1965, 24–7, and David E. Aune, *The New Testament and its Literary Environment*, Cambridge 1988, 204ff.
33. II Peter 3.15–16.

12. *Towards an Adult Christianity*

1. Dio Cassius, *Roman History*, LVII, 14, and Suetonius, *Domitian*, 15.
2. Cf. Pliny the Younger, *Letters*, X, 96–97.
3. Thus the establishment of Christianity beyond the Euphrates, in Osrhoene and Adiabene, which could date from these years, is only the object of

legends (cf. the one related by Eusebius in his *Church History* I,13).

4. Didache 1–6.
5. Didache 7–10.
6. Didache 11–15.
7. For the Didache see either the edition of the *Apostolic Fathers* by Kirsopp Lake in the Loeb Classical Library, London and New York 1912, or by M. Staniforth in *Early Christian Writings*, Penguin Classics, Harmondsworth 1989.
8. II John 1.1; III John 1.1.
9. II John 7–12.
10. III John 9–10.
11. Cf. Pierre Bonnard, *Les Épîtres johanniques*, Geneva 1983, 119–38.
12. II Clement 59.22–61.
13. II Clement 62–65.
14. The text can be found in the works mentioned in n.7 above.
15. Cf. his letter to the Romans.
16. Eph. 7.2; Magn. 8.2; Trall. 9.1–2; Smyrn. 1.1–2.
17. E.g. Trall. 6.1–2.
18. Magn. 10.1–3; Philad. 6.1.
19. Magn.10.1–3; Rom. 3.3; Philad. 6.1.
20. Eph. 1.3; 3.2; 5.1–3; 6.1; Magn. 2–4; 6.1 – 7.1; 13.1–2; Trall. 2.1; 3.1–2; 7.1–2; Philad. 1.1–ch.4; 8.1–9.11; 12.2; Smyrn. 8.1 to 9.1; Polycarp 1.1–3.2; 5.2–3.
21. Eph. 4.1; Magn. 2; 3.1; 6.1–7.1; 13.1; Trall. 2.2; 3.1; 7.1; Philad. 4; 8.1; 10.2; Smyrn 8.11; 12.2; Polycarp 6.1.
22. Magn. 2; 6.1; 13.1; Trall. 2.3; 3.1; 7.2; Philad. 4; 10.2; Smyrn. 12.2; Polycarp 6.1.
23. See the edition by William Schoedel, *Ignatius of Antioch*, Hermeneia, Philadelphia 1985.
24. Polycarp 2.1; 7.1–2; 12.2.
25. Polycarp 5.23; 6.1; 11.1–4.
26. Polycarp 3.3; 4.1; 5.1; 6.2; 9 and 10; 12.1–3.
27. Polycarp 4.2; 4.3; 5.3;
28. Polycarp 12.3.
29. Polycarp 8.2 – 9.2.
30. Polycarp 12.1.
31. Polycarp 2.1; 6.1; 10.3; 11.2; 12.1.
32. The letter of Polycarp can be found in Lake (ed.), *Apostolic Fathers* (n.7), Vol.1.
33. Heb. 13.22–25.
34. Heb. 13.7, 17.
35. Heb. 10.25.
36. Heb. 10.32–34; 12.4–8.
37. Cf. Heb. 13.9–15.
38. Heb. 4.14.
39. Cf. Gen.14.17–20; Ps.110.4.
40. Heb. 10.1–18.

41. Heb. 12.22–24.
42. Though several important monographs have appeared on the letter to the Hebrews, see still Ceslas Spicq, *L'Épître aux Hébreux*, Paris 1952–53 (2 vols); in English see H.W. Attridge, Hermeneia, Philadelphia 1989.
43. Rev. 1.9.
44. Rev. 1.10–3.22.
45. See especially chs. 17 and 18.
46. See the commentary by John Sweet, *Revelation*, London and Philadelphia 1990.
47. I John 1.1–5; 2.25; 4.6, 14.
48. I John 2.1, 7–8, 12–13, 21, 26; 5.13–16.
49. I John 2.7; 3.2, 21; 4.1, 7, 11.
50. I John 2.1, 12, 18, 28; 3.7, 18; 4.4; 5.21.
51. I John 1.6–10; 2.1–3, 5, 18–19, 28; 3.1–2, 11, 14, 16, 18–24; 4.7, 9–13, 16–17, 19, 21; 5.2–3, 9,11, 14–15, 18–20.
52. I John 2.7–11; 3.11–23; 4.7–12, 19–21.
53. I John 2.15–17; 3.1–13; 4.4–5; 5.4–5, 19.
54. I John 1.7–10; 2.2–12; 3.5; 4.9–10.
55. I John 1.6–7; 2.8–10.
56. I John 2.7–8; 3.23; 5.1–4.
57. I John 2.13–14, 20–21, 27; 4.6–7; 5.15, 18–20.
58. I John 3.24; 4.1–6, 13; 5.6–8.
59. I John 1.1–2; 2.25; 3.14–15; 5.11–13, 16, 20.
60. I John 1.8, 10.
61. I John 2.22–23; 4.3.
62. I John 2.4, 9, 11; 3.8, 10, 14–15, 17; 4.20.
63. Cf. J.L. Houlden, *Commentary on the Johannine Epistles*, London and New York 1974, the bulk of which is devoted to I John.
64. John 9.22; 12.41; 16.2.
65. Cf. Acts 19.1–7.
66. John 1.15–39; 3.22–30; 4.1; 5.31–35, etc.
67. John 2.13–3.30; 5; 7.14–10.39; 12.12–50.
68. Cf. John 9.13–41; 12.42.
69. John 2.1–11.
70. John 2.13–22.
71. Cf. Matt. 23.
72. John 2.13–25; 5.1–46; 7.11–52; 8.12–59; 9.35–41; 10.22–39; 12.37–50.
73. John 7.37–39; 14.16–17, 26; 15.26; 16.13–15.
74. John 2.23–25; 3.1–12; 5.37–47; 6.14–15, 24–50, 60–66; 7.3–9, 14–36, 40–52; 8.12–20, 31–59; 10.22–39; 12.37–50.
75. John 4.46–53; 9.1–39.
76. John 4.5–42; 12.20–26.
77. John 1.35–51.
78. John 1.15–34; 3.27–36.
79. John 17.1–2, 6–19.
80. John 1.6–13.
81. John 1.25–28, 31, 33; 3.23.

82. John 1.30–33.
83. John 1.29.
84. John 1.31–34.
85. John 1.19–27; 3.27–28.
86. John 1.15–18; 1.26–27, 29–36; 3.29–36; 5.31–35.
87. John 1.35–51.
88. John 6.60–69.
89. John 6.70–71; 13.21–30.
90. John 13.1–20.
91. John 13.31–17.26.
92. John 16.8.
93. John 17.20–23.
94. John 20.21–22.
95. John 20.23.
96. John 6.51–58.
97. John 3.3–8; 4.2, 13–14.
98. John 13.34–35.
99. John 17.21–23.
100. Of a vast literature on the Fourth Gospel, in English see e.g. Oscar Cullmann, *The Johannine Circle*, London 1976, and Martin Hengel, *The Johannine Question*, London and Philadelphia 1990.

13. *Consolidation and Hellenization*

1. For the large Gnostic library discovered at Nag Hammadi in 1945, containing in particular the complete text of the Gospel of Thomas, previously known only in English, see James M. Robinson (ed.), *The Nag Hammadi Library*, Leiden ²1984.
2. Erich Fuchs and Pierre Reymond, *La Deuxième Épître de saint Pierre. L'Épître de saint Jude*, Neuchâtel and Paris 1980.
3. 1 QS 3.13–4.26.
4. The text of the Letter of Barnabas can be found in the edition by Kirsopp Lake of the *Apostolic Fathers*, Loeb Classical Library, London and New York, Vol.1.
5. The text of the Shepherd of Hermas can be found in Lake (ed.), *Apostolic Fathers* (n.4), Vol.2.
6. Hermas 1.1.
7. Hermas 14.1; 14.3.
8. Hermas 2.3.
9. Hermas 13.1–4.
10. Hermas 5.1; 6.3–7.
11. H. Hemmer and A. Picard, *Les Pères apostoliques* II, Paris 1909. The introduction to this old edition needs to be corrected on the basis of more recent publications like *Les écrits des Pères apostoliques*, with an introduction by Dominique Bertrand, 1991, 123–45.
12. The texts of Justin's *Apologies* can be found in the Ante-Nicene Library.
13. Cf. W. Schneemelcher and R. McL. Wilson (eds.), *New Testament*

Apocrypha (2 vols), Louisville and Cambridge 1991, 1992, I, 172–8, and II, 34–41.

14. Basilides, *Fragments cited in Clement of Alexandria, Stromata*, ed. O. Stählin and L. Früchtel, GCS 15, 17, Berlin 1960.
15. For Marcion see two great classic monographs: A. von Harnack, *Marcion, das Evangelium vom fremden Gott*, Leipzig ²1921; E.C. Blackman, *Marcion and his Influence*, New York and London 1950.

Conclusion

1. Takashi Kato, *La Pensée sociale de Luc-Actes,* Paris 1997, is a talented demonstration of how this fateful step was taken.

Index